WARM FRUIT BAKES
for crisp days

WARM FRUIT BAKES for crisp days

OVER 65 COMFORTING RECIPES TO WARM THE SOUL

RYLAND PETERS & SMALL

Senior Designer Iona Hoyle
Editor Rebecca Woods
Head of Production Patricia Harrington
Art Director Leslie Harrington
Editorial Director Julia Charles
Publisher Cindy Richards

Indexer Hilary Bird

This edition published in 2026
by Ryland Peters & Small
20–21 Jockey's Fields, London WC1R 4BW
www.rylandpeters.com
email: euregulations@ rylandpeters.com

Previously published in 2010, 2013, and 2020 as *Cinnamon, Spice & Warm Apple Pie*

10 9 8 7 6 5 4 3 2 1

Recipe collection compiled by Julia Charles.

ISBN: 978-1-78879-778-8

Printed in China

CIP data from the Library of Congress has been applied for. A CIP record for this book is available from the British Library.

The authorised representative in the EEA is Authorised Rep Compliance Ltd., Ground Floor, 71 Lower Baggot Street, Dublin, D02 P593, Ireland
www.arccompliance.com

FSC www.fsc.org
MIX
Paper | Supporting responsible forestry
FSC® C008047

Notes

• Both British (Metric) and American (Imperial plus US cup) measurements are given in these recipes for your convenience, however it is important to work with one set of measurements only and not alternate between the two when following a recipe.

• All spoon measurements are level unless otherwise specified.

• All eggs are medium (UK) or large (US) unless otherwise specified. Free-range eggs are recommended. Uncooked or partly cooked eggs should not be served to the very young, the very old, those with compromised immune systems or to pregnant women.

• When a recipe calls for the grated zest of lemons and limes, buy unwaxed fruit and wash well before using. If you can only find treated fruit, scrub well in warm, soapy water before using.

• Ovens should be preheated to the specified temperature. Recipes in this book were tested using a regular oven. If using a fan-assisted oven, follow the manufacturer's instructions for adjusting temperatures.

contents

introduction

What could be more enticing and take the edge off of a cold winter's day than an apple crumble warm from the oven or a blackberry cobbler, bubbling up with rich juices? Simple, delicious and cherished – these old-fashioned fruit desserts are experiencing a long overdue revival. In this collection of recipes you'll find all of your best-loved desserts in one place. Whether you are searching for the perfect ending to a dinner party or a treat to wrap up any night of the week, these quick and easy-to-prepare ideas will soon become firm favourites.

The old-time fruit desserts here have long been called by various names but what they have in common is that they are all homely recipes based on seasonal fruits that rely more on good fresh ingredients than fancy preparation. A crumble is the classic British comfort food – fruit sprinkled with a melt-in-mouth pastry crumb mix. Bettys are a classic American baked pudding made of alternate layers of sugared fruit and buttered breadcrumbs – a recipe created to make use of stale leftovers. Another iconic recipe from the States is the cobbler, which is basically stewed fruit on top of which a scone dough is dropped in lumps before baking. (It is said that the dish got its name as the cooked dough resembles cobblestones.) A clafoutis is a French dessert that comprises fresh fruit baked in a rich egg custard. The wonderfully descriptive slump is also a battered dessert but unlike clafoutis is most often cooked, or at least started, on top of the hob in a baking pan rather than in the oven. Recipes for crisps are open to interpretation but they are often a simple fruit bake topped with crumbled biscuits or pastry and baked. The curiously named pandowdy is an upside-down fruit pie with a rolled crust top, which is broken up with a spoon. Also included are great recipes for other popular fruit-based bakes such as pies, tarts and strudels, as well as some deliciously moist fork cakes.

There is nothing like a home-baked fruit pudding, so create a little nostalgia in your kitchen with one of these classic recipes.

crumbles & streusels

There is no better partner for apples than ripe, juicy blackberries. This easy dessert is simply divine served warm from the oven with a scoop of vanilla ice cream. If there's any leftover, have it with Greek-style yogurt for breakfast.

apple & blackberry crumble

Preheat the oven to 200°C (400°F) Gas 6.

Put the apples, blackberries and sugar in a bowl and use your hands to mix well. Transfer to the prepared baking dish.

To prepare the crumble topping, combine the oats, flour, sugar, almonds and cinnamon in a bowl and mix well. Add the butter. Using your fingertips, rub in the butter until the mixture resembles coarse breadcrumbs. Alternatively, use a food processor and blend carefully with the pulse button but do not over-process or you will grind the oats too finely.

Sprinkle the crumble topping evenly over the apple mixture. Bake in the preheated oven for 35–45 minutes, until the crumble is golden and the fruit is bubbling. Serve warm with vanilla ice cream.

900 g/2 lbs. mixed apple varieties, peeled, cored and chopped

450 g/1 lb. blackberries

50 g/¼ cup caster/granulated sugar

vanilla ice cream, to serve

for the crumble topping:

80 g/1 cup porridge oats

140 g/1 cup plain/all-purpose flour

80 g/½ cup light soft brown sugar

80 g/½ cup ground almonds

½ teaspoon ground cinnamon

150 g/1 stick plus 2 tablespoons unsalted butter, chilled and cubed

a medium ovenproof dish or 4–6 individual dishes, well buttered

serves 4–6

Fresh berries are so tasty and good just as they are that it's tempting not to fuss with them too much. That said, they are also very good used in a crumble. The floral aroma of blackberries can be enhanced by adding a small splash of rosewater or orange blossom essence to the berries. Keep this in mind whenever you are serving or cooking with any red berry.

blackberry crumble

375 g/12 oz. blackberries
1 tablespoon caster/granulated sugar
1 teaspoon cornflour/cornstarch

for the crumble topping:

130 g/1 cup plain/all-purpose flour
75 g/5 tablespoons unsalted butter, chilled and cubed
60 g/¼ cup light soft brown sugar
chilled cream, to serve

a medium ovenproof dish, lightly buttered

serves 4

Preheat the oven to 180°C (350°F) Gas 4.

Put the blackberries in a bowl with the caster/granulated sugar and the cornflour/cornstarch and toss to mix. Tumble the berries into the prepared baking dish and set aside for 15–20 minutes.

Put the flour and butter in a bowl and, using your fingertips, rub the butter into the flour until the mixture resembles coarse breadcrumbs. Stir in the brown sugar.

Sprinkle the crumble mixture evenly over the berries and bake in the preheated oven for 45–50 minutes, until the top is golden brown. Let the crumble cool slightly before serving with cream.

Plums have such a rich flavour when they are cooked that they need little or no other flavourings with them, except perhaps a pinch of cinnamon. You could also bake this recipe with yellow plums, greengages or mirabelles – they will all be delicious. For a special treat, toss the uncooked plums in a little damson or sloe gin.

simple plum crumble

8–10 ripe plums

4–5 tablespoons sugar

chilled cream, to serve

for the crumble topping:

75 g/5 tablespoons unsalted butter, chilled and cubed

175 g/1⅓ cups plain/all-purpose flour

a pinch of salt

50 g/¼ cup caster/granulated sugar

a medium ovenproof dish, butttered

serves 4–6

Preheat the oven to 180°C (350°F) Gas 4 and put a baking sheet on the middle shelf to heat.

Halve the plums and remove the stones/pits. Cut the halves into quarters if they are very large. Toss them with the sugar and tip them into the prepared baking dish.

To make the crumble topping, use your fingertips to rub the butter into the flour with the salt until it resembles coarse breadcrumbs. Alternatively do this in a food processor. Stir in the sugar.

Lightly scatter the crumble topping over the plums. Place the baking dish on the hot baking sheet and bake in the preheated oven for 40–45 minutes, until golden brown.

Remove from the oven and serve warm with cream.

This luscious crumble is sophisticated enough for a smart dinner party. Chocolate and pears were made for each other – here the chocolate melts and mixes with the pear juice to make a delicious sauce. Pumpernickel makes an interestingly crunchy topping, and gives the dessert a dramatic look.

pear & chocolate crumble

2–3 large not-too-ripe pears

50 g/¼ cup caster/granulated sugar

2–3 tablespoons drinking chocolate (not unsweetened cocoa) or grated dark chocolate

finely grated zest of ½ a lemon

chocolate ice cream or chilled cream, to serve

for the pumpernickel topping:

100 g/4 oz. sliced pumpernickel

100 g/4 oz. stale brown bread

4 tablespoons drinking chocolate (not unsweetened cocoa) or grated dark chocolate

50 g/½ stick unsalted butter, chilled and cubed

75 g/⅓ cup demerara sugar

a medium ovenproof dish, buttered

serves 4

Preheat the oven to 180°C (350°F) Gas 4 and put a baking sheet on the middle shelf to heat.

Peel, core and slice the pears and put them in the prepared baking dish so that they fill it by two thirds. Sprinkle the sugar, drinking chocolate and lemon zest over the top and mix well to coat the pears. Cover and set aside.

To make the crumble topping, tear up the pumpernickel and bread slices and put in the bowl of a food processor. Pulse for a minute or so until very roughly crumbed. Add the drinking chocolate, butter and sugar and pulse again for a minute or so until finer crumbs form. Do not over-process or it will form a solid lump.

Uncover the pears and sprinkle lightly and evenly with the topping mixture. Place the baking dish on the hot baking sheet and bake in the preheated oven for 25–30 minutes, until the pears are very tender and the topping is crisp.

Remove from the oven and serve warm with chocolate ice cream or cream.

Gooseberries seem to have a natural affinity with ginger. Ginger wine is a delicious tipple on its own but it really brings out the flavour of gooseberries. It's best to cook the fruit a little first to draw out the juice (as it makes the crumble too wet and sloppy) but you can reserve this liquid, warm it and and serve alongside the cooked crumble.

gooseberry & ginger crumble

900 g/2 lbs. gooseberries, topped and tailed

3 tablespoons ginger wine

125 g/generous ½ cup caster/granulated sugar

clotted or double/heavy cream, to serve

for the ginger topping:

200 g/1½ cups plain/all-purpose flour

1 teaspoon ground ginger

a pinch of salt

100 g/1 stick unsalted butter, chilled and cubed

100 g/½ cup caster/granulated sugar

a medium ovenproof dish or 4 individual dishes, well buttered

serves 4

Preheat the oven to 190°C (375°F) Gas 5 and put a baking sheet on the middle shelf to heat.

Put the gooseberries in a non-reactive saucepan, add the ginger wine and sugar and cook gently until the fruit starts to burst. Remove from the heat and tip the gooseberries into a sieve/strainer set over a clean saucepan to catch the juices. Put the gooseberries into the prepared baking dish, covering the base with a single layer. Reserve the juices for later.

To make the ginger topping, put the flour, ginger, salt and butter in the bowl of a food processor and process until it resembles coarse breadcrumbs. (Alternatively you can rub in by hand.) Tip into a mixing bowl and stir in the sugar.

Lightly sprinkle the topping evenly over the gooseberry mixture, mounding it up a little towards the centre. Place the baking dish on the hot baking sheet and bake in the preheated oven for about 25 minutes, until crisp and golden.

Remove from the oven and let cool for 5 minutes before serving with the warmed reserved juices and clotted cream.

Crumbles are normally considered to be a comforting winter dessert, but this deliciously light, nutty version makes the most of juicy summer nectarines. It takes very little time to prepare and tastes sublime with ice cream.

nectarine & pistachio crumble

6 nectarines

vanilla ice cream, to serve

for the nutty crumble topping:

70 g/½ cup shelled pistachios, coarsely chopped

50 g/⅓ cup blanched whole almonds

60 g/½ cup ground oatmeal or oat flour

50 g/½ stick unsalted butter, chilled and cubed

60 g/½ cup plain/all-purpose flour

50 g/¼ cup light soft brown sugar

a baking sheet lined with baking parchment

serves 6

Preheat the oven to 220°C (425°F) Gas 7.

To make the crumble topping, put the pistachios and almonds in a food processor and process until coarsely chopped. Transfer to a bowl. Add the oatmeal and butter and use your fingertips to rub the ingredients together until the mixture resembles coarse, wet sand. Add the flour and sugar and rub together to combine. Cover and refrigerate until needed.

Cut the nectarines in half. If the stone/pit does not come out easily, don't worry – simply slice the flesh off the fruit and drop it directly onto the prepared baking sheet. Sprinkle the crumble topping evenly over the nectarines and bake in the preheated oven for 10–15 minutes, until the fruit is soft and juicy and the topping is a soft golden colour. Serve warm with ice cream.

Christmas is definitely coming when the smell of this crumble starts to drift around the house. A classic mixture of dried fruits provides a rich base for the light crumble topping. The spicy mulled wine seeps into the fruits as they cook and plumps them up nicely. Serve this as a superior substitute for more traditional mince pies.

mulled mixed fruit crumble

350 g/12 oz. mixed dried fruits (such as raisins, sultanas/golden raisins, apples, figs, apricots and cranberries)

300 ml/1 generous cup red wine

1 small muslin/cheesecloth bag of mulling spices for wine (cinnamon, cloves and allspice)

a strip of orange zest

50 g/¼ cup caster/granulated sugar

clotted or double/heavy cream, to serve

for the spiced crumble topping:

200 g/1½ cups wholemeal/whole-wheat flour

¼ teaspoon ground mixed/apple pie spice

a pinch of salt

100 g/1 stick unsalted butter, chilled and cubed

100 g/½ cup demerera sugar

a medium ovenproof dish

serves 4

Preheat the oven to 190°C (375°F) Gas 5 and put a baking sheet on the middle shelf to heat.

Chop the dried fruits into bite-sized pieces and place in a non-reactive saucepan. Add the wine, mulling spices, orange zest and caster/granulated sugar. Heat gently, then let simmer for about 10 minutes. Set aside to cool.

Spoon the semi-cooked dried fruit into a baking dish and remove the mulling spices and orange zest.

To make the topping, put the flour, mixed/apple pie spice, salt and butter into a food processor and process until it looks like coarse breadcrumbs. (Alternatively you can rub in by hand.) Tip the mixture into a bowl and stir in the sugar.

Lightly sprinkle the topping mixture evenly over the surface of the dried fruits, mounding it up a little towards the centre. Place on the hot baking sheet and bake in the preheated oven for about 25 minutes, until crisp and golden on top.

Remove from the oven and let cool for 5 minutes before serving with clotted cream.

Rhubarb holds vivid childhood memories for most people. Whether it's of dipping young raw rhubarb sticks into sugar and munching away, or enjoying a delicious crumble with plenty of hot custard. Orange seems to draw out and temper the sharp flavour of rhubarb with delicious results.

rhubarb & orange crumble

700 g/1½ lbs. forced rhubarb
2 large oranges
a pinch of ground ginger
175 g/¾ cup golden caster/natural cane sugar
clotted or double/heavy cream, to serve

for the almond topping:

125 g/1 cup plain/all-purpose flour
a pinch of salt
55 g/⅔ cup ground almonds
125 g/1 stick unsalted butter, chilled and cubed
125 g/1 cup blanched almonds, chopped
55 g/¼ cup demerara sugar

a medium ovenproof dish

serves 4

Preheat the oven to 200°C (400°F) Gas 6 and put a baking sheet on the middle shelf to heat.

Trim the rhubarb, cut it into large chunks and put it in a large saucepan. Finely grate the zest from the oranges and add to the rhubarb. Stir in the ginger and sugar and cook over a gentle heat for a few minutes, stirring occasionally until the rhubarb begins to release its juices but is still holding its shape. Pour the rhubarb into a sieve/strainer set over a bowl to catch the juices and reserve these for later. Remove the pith from the oranges with a small sharp knife then cut out the segments between the membrane. Add to the drained rhubarb and set aside to cool completely.

To make the almond topping, put the flour, salt, ground almonds and butter into a food processor and process until it looks like coarse breadcrumbs. (Alternatively you can rub in by hand.) Tip the mixture into a bowl and stir in the chopped nuts and sugar.

Spoon the rhubarb and oranges into a baking dish. Lightly sprinkle the almond topping evenly over the surface, mounding it up a little towards the centre. Place the baking dish on the hot baking sheet and bake in the preheated oven for about 35 minutes, until crisp and golden.

Remove from the oven and let cool for 5 minutes before serving with the warmed reserved juices and cream.

Pine nuts and almonds, with their toasty flavours, add another dimension to this simple crumble. The crust is quite loose so it will need to settle before it crisps up, which is perfect because crumble is best eaten warm rather than piping hot. The brown sugar thickens the plum juices to create a caramel which bubbles up to stain the nutty crust.

nutty plum crumble

Preheat the oven to 180°C (350°F) Gas 4.

Halve the plums and remove the stones/pits, then arrange them in a single layer in a baking dish. Add the orange zest and juice. Sprinkle over 2 tablespoons of the sugar and dot over 25 g/2 tablespoons of the butter. Cover with foil and bake in the preheated oven for about 25–30 minutes, until the plums are beginning to soften.

Put the flour, ground almonds and the remaining butter in a bowl and rub it between your fingertips until it forms lumps. Stir in the almonds, pine nuts and the remaining sugar.

Remove the baking dish from the oven, discard the foil and scatter over the crumble topping. Return to the oven and bake for about 30 minutes, until the topping is golden and the juices are bubbling through. Let stand for 10 minutes to allow the crust to firm up. Serve with cream.

12 ripe plums

2–3 thick strips of zest and the freshly squeezed juice from 1 orange

75 g/⅓ cup light soft brown sugar

125 g/1 stick unsalted butter, chilled and cubed

100 g/¾ cup self-raising flour

50 g/⅓ cup ground almonds

3 tablespoons flaked/slivered almonds

3 tablespoons pine nuts

chilled cream, to serve

a medium ovenproof dish

serves 4

These little crumbles are a bit of a fiddle to make, but well worth the effort. Be very careful when transferring them from the pan to the plate – a trusty fish slice will help. They make an impressive dinner party dessert and a rather more sophisticated alternative to banoffi pie.

toffee banana crumbles

8 firm bananas
50 g/¼ cup light soft brown sugar
freshly squeezed juice of 1 lemon
chilled double/heavy cream or crème fraîche, to serve

for the coconut topping:

50 g/⅓ cup plain/all-purpose flour
50 g/⅔ cup unsweetened desiccated/dried shredded coconut
50 g/½ stick unsalted butter, chilled and cubed
25 g/2 tablespoons caster/granulated sugar

a cast-iron skillet or heavy frying pan with a heatproof handle

4 individual heatproof chef's rings (each about 7-cm/3-inches diameter)

serves 4

Preheat the oven to 190°C (375°F) Gas 5.

Trim and cut the bananas into 3-cm/1¼-inch lengths. Reserve four of the lengths for the centres of the crumbles, then slice each of the remaining ones in half lengthways. Sprinkle the brown sugar into a skillet, then place the chef's rings into the sugar. Pack each ring with an upright banana. Next, tightly surround this with the split bananas (to resemble the petals of a flower) and pour the lemon juice over the top.

To make the topping, put the flour, coconut and butter in a food processor and process until it resembles coarse breadcrumbs. (Alternatively you can rub in by hand.) Tip into a bowl and stir in the sugar.

Fill each ring to the top with the coconut topping. Transfer the skillet to the preheated oven and bake for about 25 minutes, until the crumbles are golden. Remove from the oven and slip a fish slice under each ring to lift them out of the pan and onto warmed serving plates. Carefully remove the rings and serve with the pan juices spooned around the crumbles and cream or crème fraîche.

This crumble is based on a famous Scottish dessert, combining raspberries with toasted oatmeal, whisky, heather honey and cream. If you are using frozen raspberries, there is no need to defrost them first. The oat topping packs a satisfyingly toasty crunch.

cranachan crumble

350 g/12 oz. fresh or frozen raspberries

6 tablespoons heather honey

100 ml/½ cup double/heavy cream

2 tablespoons whisky

lightly whipped double/heavy cream, to serve

for the oatmeal topping:

85 g/¾ stick unsalted butter

100 g/¾ cup fine oatmeal

100 g/1 cup rolled oats (not instant)

a medium ovenproof dish

serves 4–6

Preheat the oven to 190°C (375°F) Gas 5. Put a baking sheet on the middle shelf to heat.

Put the raspberries into an ovenproof baking dish. Drizzle with 3 tablespoons of the honey and pour in the cream and whisky.

To make the topping, melt the butter and the remaining honey in a saucepan and stir in both types of oats. Stir until they start to clump together like a crunchy breakfast cereal.

Sprinkle the oat mixture evenly over the surface of the raspberries, mounding it up a little towards the centre.

Place the baking dish on the baking sheet in the preheated oven and bake the crumble for about 20–25 minutes, until crisp and golden on top.

Let cool for 5 minutes before serving with cream.

This delicious streusel is really nice made in individual dishes or cups, but make sure they are ovenproof. Serve each guest their own little jug of cold pouring cream so that they don't feel greedy reaching over the table for more!

cranberry & orange streusel

500 g/1 lb. fresh or frozen cranberries

finely grated zest and freshly squeezed juice of 1 orange

honey, to taste

chilled single/light cream, to serve

for the streusel topping:

75 g/½ cup plain/all-purpose flour

75 g/⅓ cup light soft brown sugar

75 g/5 tablespoons unsalted butter, chilled and cubed

a medium ovenproof dish

serves 4

Preheat the oven to 220°C (425°F) Gas 7.

Put the cranberries in a saucepan with the orange juice and bring to the boil. Cook for 2 minutes then remove from the heat and sweeten to taste with honey. Pour into a baking dish and let cool.

Mix the flour, sugar and orange zest in a bowl and add the butter. Rub the butter into the dry mixture until it resembles fine breadcrumbs and is on no account greasy or oily. (Pop into a plastic bag and leave in the fridge for 20 minutes if it has become so.)

Once the cranberries are cold, sprinkle the topping evenly over the top. Bake in the preheated oven for 10 minutes, then reduce the oven temperature to 180°C (350°F) Gas 4 and bake for a further 15 minutes.

Remove from the oven and serve warm with cream.

Here the halved pears act as an edible dish. It is really important to caramelize the cut side of the pears to a dark mahogany to bring out their flavour. Don't add too much egg to the almond mix – it must be quite lumpy so that it doesn't flow out of the pears as it cooks.

bourbon pears with frangipane streusel

Preheat the oven to 190°C (375°F) Gas 5.

Halve the pears, and scoop out the cores. Melt the sugar in a heavy frying pan and cook until a good dark caramel. Splash in the bourbon, then add the pears cut-side down with the butter. Cook over medium heat for 10 minutes or until the cut side of the pears turns a rich dark brown. Remove from the heat and arrange the pears cut-side up in a baking dish. Pour the cooking juices around the pears.

To make the frangipane topping, mix the ground almonds, chopped almonds and caster/granulated sugar with a splash of bourbon and enough beaten egg until it begins to clump together. Mound this mixture on top of the baked pears and scatter with the flaked almonds. Bake in the preheated oven for 20–25 minutes, until golden.

Remove from the oven, spoon over the caramelized juices and serve warm with whipped cream or vanilla ice cream.

2 large pears

4 tablespoons sugar

4 tablespoons bourbon

100 g/1 stick unsalted butter

vanilla ice cream or whipped cream, to serve

for the frangipane topping:

100 g/1 cup ground almonds

50 g/⅓ cup chopped or nibbed almonds

150 g/⅔ cup caster/granulated sugar

an extra splash of bourbon

1 egg, beaten

50 g/½ cup flaked/slivered almonds

a medium ovenproof dish

serves 4

cobblers & more

Cranberries add a pleasing tang to this cobbler. If you can't easily find fresh cranberries, simply buy dried ones and soak them for at least one hour in warmed cranberry juice before using.

cranberry & apple cobbler

450 g/1 lb. fresh or frozen cranberries (or 200 g/½ cup dried cranberries)

450 g/1 lb. cooking apples

finely grated zest and freshly squeezed juice of 1 small orange

a pinch of ground cloves

chilled double/heavy cream, to serve

for the cobbler topping:

50 g/½ stick unsalted butter, chilled and cubed

225 g/1¾ cups self-raising flour

a pinch of salt

50 g/¼ cup caster/granulated sugar

about 150 ml/⅔ cup milk, plus extra to glaze

a medium ovenproof dish
a fluted 4–5-cm/1½–2-inch cookie cutter

serves 4

Preheat the oven to 220°C (425°F) Gas 7.

Pick over the cranberries and wash them. Peel and core the apples, then slice them thickly. Put 375 g/13 oz. of the cranberries and the apples into a saucepan with the orange zest and juice and the cloves. Poach gently for 15–20 minutes, until the fruit is juicy and tender. Set aside and let cool.

Roughly chop the remaining cranberries. Rub the butter into the flour and salt until it resembles fine breadcrumbs. Stir in the sugar and chopped cranberries. Add the milk, mixing with a blunt knife to form a fairly soft, sticky dough. Tip the dough out onto a floured work surface and roll out to a thickness of about 2 cm/¾ inch. Stamp out rounds with the cookie cutter.

Spoon the fruit into a baking dish and arrange the rounds against the edge of the dish, overlapping them slightly and leaving a gap in the centre. Brush the top of the rounds with milk. Bake in the preheated oven for 10–15 minutes, until the pastry is golden brown. Serve hot with cream.

This style of cobbler is quite similar to a French clafoutis but the batter uses more flour and has baking powder instead of eggs to lift it. Use big juicy blackberries for this recipe and the batter will be marbled with their colour.

blackberry cobbler

225 g/1¾ cups plain/all-purpose flour
¼ teaspoon mixed spice/apple pie spice (optional)
150 g/⅔ cup caster/granulated sugar
a large pinch of salt
4 teaspoons baking powder
250 ml/1 cup milk
½ teaspoon vanilla extract
50 g/½ stick unsalted butter
675 g/1½ lbs. fresh or frozen blackberries
chilled cream or hot custard, to serve

a large metal baking pan

serves 4–6

Preheat the oven to 180°C (350°F) Gas 4.

Sift the flour, mixed spice/apple pie spice (if using) sugar, salt and baking powder into a bowl. Gradually whisk in the milk and vanilla extract to give a thick batter. Let sit for 15 minutes.

Melt the butter over a gentle heat in a shallow, metal baking pan. Give the rested batter a quick stir, then pour the batter into the pan over the melted butter. Don't worry if the butter floats around and mingles with the batter at this stage.

Immediately scatter the blackberries over the batter and transfer the cobbler to the preheated oven. Bake for about 55 minutes, until the batter has puffed up and set.

Serve warm with cream or custard.

This American classic should be eaten soon after baking because the cobbler dough soaks up the fruit juices upon standing, but that doesn't mean you should overlook any leftovers as a breakfast option the next day!

peach cobbler

Preheat the oven to 190°C (375°F) Gas 5.

Cut the peaches in half, remove the stones/pits, then cut each half into 3 slices. Arrange the slices in a baking dish, sprinkle with the flour and toss well to coat evenly. Add the lemon juice and honey and stir. Set aside.

To make the topping, put the cream and crème fraîche in a large bowl and stir well. Put the flour, sugar, baking powder, bicarbonate of soda/baking soda and salt in a separate bowl and mix well. Add the butter and rub in with your fingertips until the mixture resembles coarse breadcrumbs. Using a fork, stir in the cream mixture until blended – use your hands at the end if necessary, the mixture should be sticky, thick and not willing to blend easily.

Drop spoonfuls of the mixture on top of the peaches, leaving gaps to expose the fruit. Sprinkle sugar liberally over the top. Bake in the preheated oven for 25–35 minutes, until golden.

Serve warm with cream or vanilla ice cream.

6 not-too-ripe peaches

1 tablespoon plain/all-purpose flour

1 tablespoon freshly squeezed lemon juice

3 tablespoons honey

chilled cream or vanilla ice cream, to serve

for the cobbler topping:

125 ml/½ cup double/heavy cream

5 tablespoons crème fraîche or soured cream

165 g/1¼ cups plain/all-purpose flour

50 g/¼ cup sugar, plus extra for sprinkling

1 teaspoon baking powder

¼ teaspoon bicarbonate of soda/baking soda

a pinch of salt

4 tablespoons unsalted butter, chilled and cut into pieces

2–3 tablespoons sugar, for sprinkling

a large ovenproof dish

serves 6

This easy recipe is just as good made with raspberries, blackberries or blueberries. For a light scone topping, use your hands to shape the dough (a rolling pin is too heavy for such a light mixture). The walnuts and brown sugar become pleasingly crisp and contrast well with the airy scones.

raspberry & apple crispy cobbler

5 red eating apples
500 g/1 lb. raspberries
1 tablespoon caster/granulated sugar
icing/confectioners' sugar, for dusting
whipped cream, to serve

for the cobbler topping:

250 g/2 cups self-raising flour
½ teaspoon salt
3 teaspoons baking powder
1 tablespoon caster/granulated sugar
50 g/½ stick unsalted butter, chilled and cubed
75 ml/⅓ cup milk mixed with 75 ml/⅓ cup water
1 egg
1 tablespoon single/light cream
2 tablespoons coarsely chopped walnut pieces
1 tablespoon brown sugar

a medium ovenproof dish
a 6-cm/2-inch fluted cookie cutter

serves 4–6

Preheat the oven to 220°C (425°F) Gas 7.

Peel, core and thinly slice the apples. Put the apples and raspberries in a baking dish, sprinkle with the sugar and toss gently to coat the fruit in sugar.

To make the topping, sift the flour, salt and baking powder into a mixing bowl, then stir in the caster/granulated sugar. Rub in the butter with your fingertips until the mixture resembles fine breadcrumbs.

Put the milk and water mixture in a separate bowl. Add the egg and beat well. Make a well in the flour mixture, then pour in the egg mixture. Using a palette knife, draw the mixture lightly together to form a soft dough.

Turn the dough out onto a floured work surface and quickly and lightly knead the dough until smooth. Form into a ball, then press out evenly and lightly with the flat of your hand to a thickness of about 1.5 cm/½ inch. Stamp out 8 rounds with the cookie cutter, then arrange them down the sides or around the edge of the baking dish (depending on the shape of your dish), on top of the fruit, leaving a space in the centre so they will cook evenly. Brush with the cream and sprinkle with the walnuts and brown sugar.

Bake in the preheated oven for 5 minutes. Reduce the oven temperature to 200°C (400°F) Gas 6 and bake for a further 20 minutes, until the scones are well risen, golden brown and crisp with a light, fluffy centre. Dust with icing/confectioners' sugar and serve with whipped cream.

Dark bubbling blueberries hide under a light cobbled crust of lemony polenta cake. The secret of this dish is not to spoon the blobs of topping mixture too close together – leaving a little space around each one allows the fruit to bubble up through the gaps.

blueberry & lemon cobbler

675 g/1½ lbs. blueberries

120 g/1 stick unsalted butter, at room temperature

125 g/scant ⅔ cup caster/granulated sugar

finely grated zest and freshly squeezed juice of 1 lemon

100 ml/½ cup sour cream

75 g/½ cup plain/all-purpose flour

75 g/½ cup fine polenta

3 teaspoons baking powder

½ teaspoon salt

2 tablespoons honey

vanilla ice cream, to serve

a medium ovenproof dish, buttered

serves 4

Preheat oven to 180°C (350°F) Gas 4.

Spread the blueberries out in a baking dish. Cream all but 1 generous tablespoon of the butter with 75 g/⅓ cup of the sugar and the lemon zest, until pale and fluffy. Beat in the sour cream. Sift the flour with the polenta, baking powder and salt and fold into the cream mixture. Dot small spoonfuls of the mixture over the blueberries in a very random manner, until the top of the dish has been covered, leaving about 2.5 cm/1 inch space around each one. (This will give the dish its 'cobbled' look, and the juices from the fruit will bubble up around the dough.) Bake in the preheated oven for about 20 minutes, until the top is firm. While the cobbler is baking, prepare the butter mixture for the crust.

Put the remaining butter in a small saucepan with the honey, lemon juice and the remaining sugar and melt over low heat. Remove the cobbler from the oven and pour this mixture over the crust.

Increase the oven temperature to 190°C (375°F) Gas 5. Return the cobbler to the oven and cook for a further 15–20 minutes, until golden. Serve warm with vanilla ice cream.

These cheeky little cobblers will raise a smile as you bring them to the table. Use deep ramekins to achieve the impressive starry effect. They look spectacular and taste just as good as they look!

pear, maple & pecan cobblers

4 small ripe pears

finely grated zest and freshly squeezed juice of ½ a lemon

4 tablespoons pure maple syrup

50 g/½ cup roughly chopped pecan nuts

double/heavy cream or Greek-style yogurt, to serve

for the cobbler topping:

50 g/½ stick unsalted butter, chilled and cubed

225 g/1¾ cups self-raising flour

a pinch of salt

3 tablespoons maple syrup

200 ml/scant 1 cup milk

a 4–5-cm/1½–2-inch cookie cutter
4 individual ovenproof ramekins or similar

serves 4

Preheat the oven to 220°C (425°F) Gas 7.

Peel and core the pears, then slice them thickly lengthways. Put them in a saucepan with the lemon zest and juice and the maple syrup. Poach gently for 10 minutes until the fruit is almost tender. Set aside.

To make the topping, use your fingertips to rub the butter into the flour and salt until it resembles fine breadcrumbs. Stir the maple syrup into the milk and add 150 ml/⅔ cup only of this mixture to the flour, mixing with a blunt knife to form a fairly soft, sticky dough. Tip the dough out onto a floured work surface and roll out to a thickness of about 2 cm/¾ inch. Stamp out rounds with the cookie cutter.

Arrange the pear slices around the edge of the ramekins like a star, with the thicker ends in the centre of the dish and the thinner ends pointing upwards out of the dishes. Spoon the juice evenly over the pears and anchor them with a round of cobbler dough placed lightly in the centre (the pears should poke out all around the dough). Brush the top of the cobblers with the remaining milk and sprinkle with the chopped pecans.

Carefully transfer the ramekins to a baking sheet and bake in the preheated oven for 10–15 minutes, until the dough is puffed and golden brown, and the pears just browning at their tips. Serve hot with cream or Greek yogurt.

A truly decadent dessert for cold winter days. The sugar melts into the cream around the bananas, making a rich and sticky sauce. Cutting the topping into little rounds helps it to cook faster and looks very decorative. You could try making other shapes – such as hearts or flowers – using a variety of cookie cutters.

molasses banana cobbler

4 medium bananas

150 ml/⅔ cup double/heavy cream or canned evaporated milk

2 tablespoons muscovado/dark soft brown sugar

chilled cream or vanilla ice cream, to serve

for the scone topping:

225 g/1¾ cups self-raising flour

a pinch of salt

55 g/½ stick unsalted butter, chilled and cubed

25 g/2 tablespoons caster/granulated sugar

½ teaspoon ground cinnamon

3 tablespoons black treacle/dark molasses

150 ml/⅔ cup milk, plus extra for glazing

a 3-cm/1¼-inch cookie cutter
a medium ovenproof dish

serves 4

Preheat the oven to 220°C (425°F) Gas 7.

Peel the bananas and slice thickly. Arrange in a baking dish. Mix the cream with the muscovado/dark brown sugar and pour this mixture over the bananas.

To make the scone topping, sift the flour and salt into a bowl and rub in the butter. Stir in the caster/granulated sugar and cinnamon. Combine the treacle/molasses and milk, whisking with a fork until the treacle/molasses has dissolved. Quickly pour the treacle/molasses mixture into the flour mixture and mix to form a soft dough. Tip the dough out onto a floured work surface and knead briefly until smooth. Use the flat of your hand to pat out to a thickness of 2 cm/¾ inch. Stamp out as many rounds as you can with the cookie cutter, re-rolling the trimmings as necessary. Use these to cover the bananas.

Brush with a little milk and bake in the preheated oven for 15–20 minutes, until the scones are well-risen and golden brown on top. Cover with a piece of foil if the scones are cooking too quickly and the banana is still raw.

Serve warm with cream or vanilla ice cream.

Rosewater adds a delicate flavour to these pretty individual cobblers. Freezing the raspberries first makes it easier to set them into the dough but keep half unfrozen to pile on top of the cobblers for decoration.

little raspberry & rose cobblers

petals from 2 pink or red roses, washed and dried (optional)

50 g/½ stick unsalted butter, chilled and cubed

225 g/1¾ cups self-raising flour

a pinch of salt

50 g/¼ cup caster/granulated or vanilla sugar

about 150 ml/⅔ cup milk

1 tablespoon rosewater extract

600 g/1¼ lbs. raspberries, half of them frozen

icing/confectioners' sugar, for dusting

chilled cream, to serve

a 4-hole, non-stick muffin pan or 4 individual silicone muffin cups or similar

serves 4

Preheat the oven to 220°C (425°F) Gas 7.

Select the most attractive rose petals and put these to one side to use as decoration. Shred the remaining ones. Use your fingertips to rub the butter into the flour and salt until it resembles fine breadcrumbs. Stir in the sugar and shredded rose petals.

Combine the milk and rosewater extract and pour into the flour mixture, mixing with a palette knife to form a fairly soft and sticky dough. Tip out onto a floured work surface and roll out to a thickness of about 1 cm/½ inch. Stamp out 4 rounds that will fill the holes in your muffin pan.

Place the rounds gently in the muffin pan and carefully push the frozen raspberries into the cobbler dough. Dust with icing/confectioners' sugar and bake in the preheted oven for 10–15 minutes, until the dough is risen and golden brown. Let the cobblers cool in the pan for a few minutes before carefully lifting out. Serve warm with the remaining raspberries, a scattering of rose petals, a dusting of icing/confectioners' sugar and cream for pouring.

This deliciouly fruity cobbler is covered with tiny lemon-flavoured dumplings. You can use whatever berries are available but frozen mixed red berries are convenient and work very well.

berry cobbler

900 g/2 lbs. mixed summer berries (raspberries, blueberries, strawberries, blackberries, blackcurrants, cherries, etc)

3 tablespoons crème de cassis (optional)

3 tablespoons sugar

chilled single/light cream, to serve

for the lemon cobbler topping:

50 g/½ stick unsalted butter, chilled and cubed

225 g/1¾ cups self-raising flour

a pinch of salt

75 g/⅓ cup caster/granulated sugar

finely grated zest of 2 lemons and freshly squeezed juice of 1 lemon

50 ml/scant ¼ cup milk

a medium ovenproof dish

serves 4–6

Preheat the oven to 200°C (400°F) Gas 6.

Pick over the berries, discarding any really soft or bruised fruits. Mix them with the crème de cassis (if using) and sugar and transfer to a baking dish.

Rub the butter into the flour and salt until it resembles fine breadcrumbs. Stir in two thirds of the sugar and the lemon zest. Add the milk to the flour mixture, stirring with a blunt knife to form a fairly soft and sticky dough. Tip the dough out onto a floured work surface and knead lightly. Roll into a long thin sausage and using scissors, snip off little hazelnut-sized pieces. Scatter these lightly over the berries.

Mix the lemon juice with the remaining sugar and liberally brush this mixture all over the dumplings. Bake in the preheated oven for 15 minutes, until the scones are golden brown and the fruit bubbling. Serve hot with cream.

A pandowdy is made with a sweet dough baked on top of fruit, the crust being 'dowdied' by pushing it into the wonderfully fruity juices to soften it before serving. It can also be served upside down like a tarte tatin (see page 117).

plum & hazelnut pandowdy

900 g/2 lbs. plums

125 g/½ cup light soft brown sugar

½ teaspoon ground cinnamon

finely grated zest and freshly squeezed juice of 1 small orange

40 g/3 tablespoons unsalted butter, chilled and cubed

chilled cream, to serve

for the pandowdy crust:

250 g/2 cups plain/all-purpose flour

3 tablespoons caster/granulated sugar, plus extra for dusting

1 tablespoon baking powder

100 g/1 stick unsalted butter, chilled and cubed

75 g/2⅔ oz. finely ground hazelnuts

about 200 ml/generous ⅔ cup single/light cream

a cast-iron frying pan, skillet or heavy baking pan (about 26–28 cm/10–11 inches diameter)

serves 6

Preheat the oven to 220°C (425°F) Gas 7.

Halve the plums and slice them thickly. Put them in a bowl and add the soft brown sugar, cinnamon, orange zest and juice. Stir to combine then tip the plums into a cast-iron skillet. Dot with the cubes of butter. Set aside.

To make the pandowdy crust, sift the flour, sugar and baking powder into a mixing bowl. Use your fingertips to rub the butter into the flour until the mixture resembles coarse breadcrumbs. Mix in the ground hazelnuts. Stir in all but a couple of tablespoons of the cream with a palette knife, until the mixture comes together to form a sticky dough. Tip the dough out onto a floured work surface and knead very lightly until smooth.

Working quickly, roll the dough out to a circle 0.5 cm/¼ inch thick and 1 cm/½ inch wider than the skillet. With the help of the rolling pin, lift the dough over the fruit and over the edge of the pan. (Do not press the crust onto the sides of the pan.) Make a couple of slits in the dough to allow steam to escape. Brush with the remaining cream and dust with sugar.

Put the pan on a baking sheet to catch any leaking juices and bake in the preheated oven for 10 minutes, then reduce the oven temperature to 180°C (350°F) Gas 4 and loosely cover the pandowdy with foil. Return to the oven and bake for a further 35–40 minutes, until the crust is golden.

Remove from the oven and 'dowdy' the crust by sharply pushing it under the surface of bubbling fruit with a large spoon. Serve warm with cream.

This is a traditional dessert from the British West Country – little known, but highly deserving of a larger audience. It is simplicity itself to make using a food processor and uses basic ingredients.

apple dappy

450 g/1 lb. tart eating apples, such as Cox's or Braeburn, peeled, cored and diced

freshly squeezed juice of ½ a lemon

2 tablespoons sugar

1 tablespoon unsalted butter

clotted or double/heavy cream, to serve

for the pastry:

200 g/1½ cups plain/all-purpose flour

1 teaspoon baking powder

1 teaspoon bicarbonate of soda/baking soda

a pinch of salt

60 g/½ stick unsalted butter

2 tablespoons sugar

2 tablespoons clotted or double/heavy cream

125 ml/½ cup milk

caster/granulated sugar, for sprinkling

a small square or circular baking pan, lined with baking parchment and lightly buttered

serves 7

Put the apples in a saucepan with the lemon juice, sugar and butter and cook, uncovered, over medium heat until softened. Remove from the heat and set aside to cool.

Preheat the oven to 220°C (425°F) Gas 7.

In the bowl of a food processor, combine the flour, baking powder, bicarbonate of soda/baking soda and salt and pulse a few times to blend. Add the butter and sugar and pulse until the mixture resembles fine breadcrumbs. Leave the motor on and add the cream and half of the milk. The dough should be soft and sticky. If it is too stiff, add the remaining milk.

Transfer the dough to a floured surface. You need to roll it out to a rectangle measuring 20 x 30 cm/8 x 12 inches and it should be almost exactly that, not more.

Spread the cooled apple mixture over the dough and roll up from a long end, as you would a Swiss/jelly roll. Mark 7 equal pieces on the roll, then cut into slices using a sharp knife. Arrange the slices, cut-side-up in the prepared baking pan, with one in the centre and the others around it. (They should not actually touch as the dough will expand during baking.)

Sprinkle generously with sugar and bake in the preheated oven for 20–25 minutes, until puffed and golden. Let cool slightly and serve warm with cream.

bettys & crisps

If you have the patience, you can crack the apricot kernels and take out the nuts inside. These are very like bitter almonds, and are a fantastic addition when chopped and toasted with the breadcrumbs.

buttered apricot betty

Preheat the oven to 190°C (375°F) Gas 5.

Halve the fresh apricots and remove the stones/pits (or drain the canned apricots and pat dry.) Arrange a layer of apricots on the bottom of the pie dish.

Reserve 4–6 tablespoons of breadcrumbs for the top. Sprinkle some of the rest of the breadcrumbs over the apricots in the baking dish, and dot with some of the butter. Put in some more apricots and repeat these alternate layers until all the apricots and breadcrumbs are used up. Use the reserved breadcrumbs for the final top layer.

Warm the syrup with the orange juice, and pour this over the top. Sprinkle with sugar and dot with the remaining butter.

Place the pie dish in a roasting pan and pour in enough boiling water to come half way up the sides of the dish. Bake in the preheated oven for 45 minutes, until the apricots are soft and the top crisp and brown. Serve warm with cream.

675 g/1 lb. 8 oz. fresh apricots or 3 x 400-g/14-oz. cans apricots in juice (not syrup)

100 g/1 stick unsalted butter, cubed

150 g/3 cups fresh breadcrumbs, lightly toasted

2 tablespoons golden/light corn syrup

100 ml/scant ½ cup fresh orange juice

50 g/¼ cup caster/granulated sugar

chilled cream, to serve

a medium deep pie or soufflé dish, buttered

a large roasting pan

serves 4

Pineapple, rum and coconut – three flavours that are just made for each other. Blocks of sweetened coconut cream are perfect for grating into desserts, as you can use just the amount you like, and the rest keeps for ages in a plastic bag.

pineapple rum betty with coconut

1 medium pineapple

75 g/1 cup unsweetened desiccated/dried shredded coconut

75 g/3 oz. Madeira cake/vanilla pound cake or similar, crumbed

75-g/3-oz. piece of creamed coconut block, grated

75 g/¾ stick unsalted butter

100 g/4 oz. macadamia nuts, roughly chopped

2 tablespoons golden/light corn syrup

100 ml/scant ½ cup dark or golden rum

chilled cream, to serve

a medium deep pie or soufflé dish, buttered

a large roasting pan

serves 6

Preheat the oven to 190°C (375°F) Gas 5.

Cut the top and bottom off the pineapple, then cut off the skin, removing the 'eyes' using the tip of a potato peeler. Cut into quarters and then take out the hard core. Slice thinly.

Spread the coconut evenly over a baking sheet and toast in the preheated oven for about 5 minutes, until pale golden brown. Mix with the crumbed cake and half of the grated creamed coconut.

Place a layer of the sliced pineapple in the prepared pie dish. Reserve 4–6 tablespoons of the toasted coconut mixture for the top. Sprinkle some of the rest of the coconut mix over the pineapple and dot with butter. Add another layer of pineapple and repeat these alternate layers until all the pineapple and coconut mixture are used up (reserve a little of the butter for the top). Combine the reserved coconut mix with the chopped macadamia nuts and use this for the final top layer.

Warm the syrup with the rum, and pour this over the top. Sprinkle with the remaining grated creamed coconut and dot with the remaining butter. Place the pie dish in a roasting pan and pour in enough boiling water to come half way up the sides of the dish. Bake in the preheated oven for 35–40 minutes, until the pineapple is soft and the top crisp and brown. If the top browns too much, lay a piece of foil loosely on top. Serve warm with cream.

This is a traditional American recipe with very humble origins. It is always made with apples but not necessarily dried cranberries. Just like English bread pudding, it is an economic way to use up stale bread but it tastes even better if you use fresh white bread or even brioche.

apple betty with dried cranberries

Preheat the oven to 190°C (375°F) Gas 5.

Combine the apples, cinnamon, orange zest, apple juice and cranberries in a bowl. Toss gently with your hands to mix and set aside.

In a separate bowl, combine the breadcrumbs and melted butter and mix well. Spread about one-third of the buttered breadcrumbs in the bottom of the prepared pie dish. Add the chopped pecans and sugar to the remaining breadcrumbs and mix to combine.

Put half of the apple mixture on top of the breadcrumbs in the pie dish. Top with half the breadcrumb and pecan mixture and top this with the remaining apple mixture. Finish with the remainder of the breadcrumb and pecan mixture. Dot with the butter and bake in the preheated oven for 30–40 minutes, until golden and crisp. Serve warm with whipped cream.

900 g/2 lbs. tart eating apples, such as Cox's or Granny Smith, peeled, cored and diced

1 teaspoon ground cinnamon

1 tablespoon finely grated orange zest

75 ml/⅓ cup fresh apple or orange juice

100 g/⅔ cup dried cranberries

375 g/3 cups white breadcrumbs

85 g/⅔ stick unsalted butter, melted

80 g/⅔ cup shelled pecans, chopped

75 g/½ cup light soft brown sugar

2 tablespoons unsalted butter, cut into pieces

whipped cream, to serve

a medium deep pie or soufflé dish, well buttered

a large roasting pan

serves 4–6

A cheat's way of making caramel is to melt caramels in butter, as this takes away all the worry of caramelizing sugar. Adding polenta or cornmeal to this crisp topping gives it a lovely crunch. It looks very homely baked in a heavy cast-iron pan but an ordinary ovenproof dish is fine too.

caramel apple crisp

6 tart eating apples, such as Cox's or Granny Smith, peeled, cored and diced

freshly squeezed juice of ½ a lemon

50 g/½ stick unsalted butter

100 g/4 oz. hard caramel sweets/candies, crushed or chopped

a pinch of ground cinnamon

chilled crème fraîche or vanilla ice cream, to serve

for the oat crisp topping:

85 g/½ cup fine polenta

85 g/¾ cup rolled oats (not instant)

80 g/¾ stick unsalted butter, melted

130 g/½ cup demerara sugar

an ovenproof cast-iron skillet or heavy frying pan

serves 6

Preheat the oven to 190°C (375°F) Gas 5.

Core and thickly slice the apples and toss them with the lemon juice. Melt the butter in a heavy cast-iron skillet, then add the crushed caramel sweets/candies. Stir until melted, add the apples and cinnamon and toss well to coat in the buttery caramel. Set aside.

To make the oat crisp topping, put the polenta, oats and sugar in a bowl and mix well. Stir in the melted butter and work through the mixture with your fingertips until it resembles coarse breadcrumbs.

Lightly sprinkle the topping mixture evenly over the surface of the apples, mounding it up a little towards the centre. Bake in the preheated oven for 40 minutes, until browned and crisp. Serve warm with crème fraîche or vanilla ice cream.

This is a very useful recipe for when nectarines are slightly hard, as cooking them softens the flesh and brings out the flavour. Ginger goes particularly well with this fruit so ginger cookies are used here but if they are not available, simply substitute them with your favourite crunchy cookie and add a good pinch of ground ginger to the topping mixture.

nectarine & ginger crisp

6 medium nectarines

2 tablespoons finely chopped stem ginger

75 ml/scant ⅓ cup fresh apple juice

50 g/¼ cup caster/granulated sugar

vanilla ice cream or chilled cream, to serve

for the ginger crisp topping:

100 g/1 stick unsalted butter, melted

200 g/7 oz. ginger nut biscuits/gingersnap cookies, crushed

100 g/½ cup demerera sugar

a medium ovenproof dish

serves 4

Preheat the oven to 190°C (375°F) Gas 5. Put a baking sheet on the middle shelf to heat.

Halve the nectarines and remove the stones/pits, then slice or chop them. Tip them into a baking dish and mix with the apple juice, chopped ginger and sugar.

To make the ginger topping, melt the butter in a saucepan and stir in the crushed biscuits/cookies and sugar until the mixture resembles coarse breadcrumbs.

Lightly sprinkle the topping mixture evenly over the surface of the nectarines, mounding it up a little towards the centre.

Place the baking dish on top of the hot baking sheet and bake in the preheated oven about 25 minutes, until crisp and golden on top. Serve warm with vanilla ice cream or cream.

This is a back-to-front crumble. The crumble and mango are baked separately, then served together for maximum crunch. You can prepare the topping in bulk and store it in an airtight container so that you can make a really exotic dessert at a moment's notice. Do serve coconut ice cream with this, if you can find it.

mango & coconut macaroon crisp

2 ripe mangoes

finely grated zest and freshly squeezed juice of 1 lime

vanilla or coconut ice cream, to serve

for the coconut macaroon topping:

2 tablespoons wholemeal/whole-wheat flour

40 g/3 tablespoons unsalted butter

40 g/½ cup unsweetened desiccated/dried shredded coconut

80 g/3 oz. coconut macaroon biscuits/cookies

40 g/3 tablespoons demerara sugar

4 small, ovenproof dishes

serves 4

Preheat the oven to 200°C (400°F) Gas 6.

Peel the mangoes with a potato peeler. Slice the sides from the mangoes as near to the stone/pit as possible, then slice or chop the flesh, including any still clinging to the stones/pits. Toss this with the lime zest and juice and spoon into the 4 baking dishes (these must be shallow, as the mango needs to go into something that heats through quite quickly). Put them on a baking sheet and cook in the preheated oven for about 15 minutes, while you make the topping.

To make the topping, rub the flour, butter and coconut together until it resembles coarse breadcrumbs. Lightly crush the macaroon biscuits/cookies in a plastic bag, then stir these into the coconut mixture along with the sugar. Spread out onto a non-stick baking sheet and put in the oven with the mango. Toast the topping for 10–15 minutes, until crisp. Remove both sheets from the oven and sprinkle the toasted coconut macaroon topping over the hot mango.

Serve immediately with coconut or vanilla ice cream.

Some cooks like to remove the skins from the peaches before cooking them, but keeping them on here will add colour and texture to the finished dish. This can be made in individual shallow bowls or in one big dish, as you prefer. As it is quite buttery, it's best to serve it with any type of cream, except ice cream.

peach & amaretti crisp

Preheat the oven to 190°C (375°F) Gas 5. Put a baking sheet on the middle shelf to heat.

Cut the peaches in half, remove the stones/pits, then cut the peach halves into quarters. Toss with the Amaretto liqueur, if using. Arrange the peaches in a baking dish, cut-side up and in a single layer.

Roughly crush the amaretti biscuits/cookies in a plastic bag using a rolling pin. Mix the ginger syrup and egg yolk together and stir or lightly rub into the crushed biscuits until the mixture looks quite lumpy and rough. Stir in the chopped ginger.

Scatter the mixture over the peaches and dot with butter. Transfer the dish to the hot baking sheet and bake in the preheated oven for 20–25 minutes, until the peaches are tender and the amaretti topping is brown and crisp. Serve warm with crème fraîche or cream.

4–6 large, firm but ripe peaches or nectarines

2 tablespoons Amaretto di Saronno liqueur or similar (optional)

chilled crème fraîche or double/heavy cream, to serve

for the amaretti topping:

250 g/9 oz. amaretti (or ratafia) biscuits/cookies

1 egg yolk

2 tablespoons finely chopped stem ginger plus 2 tablespoons of the syrup

75 g/¾ stick unsalted butter, chilled and cubed

a medium ovenproof dish

serves 4

There is a dessert in south-west France called Pastis Gascon, which is essentially a buttery, hand-made filo/phyllo pastry apple or prune tart with a feather-light topping of sugar-dusted filo/phyllo pastry, suffused with local Armagnac. This recipe re-interprets the traditional recipe and makes it into a type of fruit crisp.

apple, prune & armagnac crisp

4 sheets filo/phyllo pastry, thawed if frozen
100 g/1 stick unsalted butter, melted
4 eating apples
16 ready-to-eat stoned/pitted prunes
2–3 tablespoons Armagnac or Cognac
3 tablespoons caster/granulated sugar
finely grated zest of 1 lemon
icing/confectioners' sugar, to dust
hot custard or chilled cream, to serve

a medium ovenproof dish

serves 4

Preheat the oven to 190°C (375°F) Gas 5.

Lay the filo/phyllo pastry out on a clean work surface and brush with the melted butter. Leave to set and dry out for 15–20 minutes.

Meanwhile, peel, core and slice the apples and quarter the prunes. Toss them together in a bowl with the Armagnac, sugar and the lemon zest. Pile the fruit into a baking dish, cover with foil and bake in the preheated oven for 20 minutes.

Scrunch the pastry up so that it rips and tears and breaks into small rags. Remove the apple and prune mixture from the oven and lightly scatter the filo/phyllo pieces on top, making sure it looks quite ragged and spiky. Return to the oven to bake for a further 20 minutes, until golden brown. Dust with icing/confectioners' sugar and serve warm with custard or cream.

clafoutis, slumps & puddings

Traditionally, this classic French dish is made using the first cherries of the season, but it is equally lovely when prepared using other stone fruits such as small peaches, nectarines or apricots. The best thing about this recipe is that the batter can be made the day before, refrigerated overnight then poured over the fruit and baked when you are ready for dessert.

cherry clafoutis

100 g/1 cup blanched almonds

1 vanilla bean, split lengthways

3 tablespoons plain/all-purpose flour

225 g/1¼ cups caster/granulated sugar

4 eggs

2 egg yolks

250 ml/1 cup single/light cream

250 g/9 oz. cherries, halved and stoned/pitted

vanilla ice cream, to serve

a medium, shallow ovenproof dish

serves 4

Preheat the oven to 220°C (425°F) Gas 7.

Spread the almonds out on a baking sheet and toast in the preheated oven for 6–8 minutes, until lightly golden. Let cool.

Put the cooled almonds in a food processor. Use the tip of a small sharp knife to scrape the seeds from the vanilla bean directly into the food processor. Process until the mixture resembles a coarse meal. Add the flour and sugar and process just to mix. Add the eggs, egg yolks and cream and process again until you have a smooth, thick batter. Transfer to a bowl, cover and refrigerate until needed.

Arrange the cherry halves in the bottom of the baking dish. Carefully pour the batter over the cherries. If need be, rearrange the cherries to evenly distribute.

Cook in the preheated oven for 25 minutes, until the clafoutis is puffed up and golden brown. Let cool for a few minutes before serving – the clafoutis will sink during this time. Serve hot with vanilla ice cream.

This delicious dessert is ideal for entertaining because it looks fantastic but is very easy to prepare. Simply make the batter and prepare the fruit in advance, then combine the two and put in the oven at the start of the meal. It will be done just when you are ready to serve.

pear & fig clafoutis

3 ripe pears
3 ripe figs
200 ml/¾ cup crème fraîche
200 ml/¾ cup milk
3 eggs
125 g/¾ cup caster/granulated sugar
2 tablespoons ground almonds
½ teaspoon ground cinnamon
icing/confectioners' sugar, to dust
chilled single/light cream, to serve

a large, shallow ovenproof dish, well buttered

serves 4–6

Preheat the oven to 200°C (400°F) Gas 6.

Peel and core the pears and cut into quite large pieces. Trim the stem ends from the figs and cut into slightly smaller pieces. If there is too much white on the fig skins, trim this off. Arrange the fruit in the prepared baking dish, distributing it evenly. Set aside.

Combine the crème fraîche, milk, eggs, sugar, almonds and cinnamon in a large mixing bowl and beat well to combine.

Pour the batter evenly over the fruit and bake in the preheated oven for about 35–45 minutes, until puffed and golden. Let cool slightly and dust with icing/confectioners' sugar just before serving. Serve warm with cream.

The word slump perfectly describes the sloppy batter which covers the seasonal fruit in this satisfying dessert. Normally the fruit is on the bottom and the thick batter spooned or poured roughly over the top but if you like to see more fruit, pour the batter in first, then push in the fruit and it works very well. You can use any juicy fruits and berries are really good too. Pine nuts can be substituted for the almonds if liked – simply sprinkle them all over the batter.

apricot & almond slump

Preheat the oven to 190°C (375°F) Gas 5.

Halve the apricots, remove the stones/pits and mix with two thirds of the sugar. Set aside until needed.

Sift the flour, baking powder, salt and remaining sugar into a bowl. Stir in the ground almonds, the milk and melted butter and whisk until smooth and thick. Pour the batter into the prepared baking pan, then push in the apricots cut-side up but in a higgledy-piggledy manner and slightly at an angle all over. Place a whole almond inside each apricot where the stone/pit once was.

Bake in the preheated oven for 25–30 minutes, until risen and golden. Let cool slightly before serving with vanilla ice cream.

600 g/1 lb. 5 oz. apricots

150 g/¾ cup golden caster/natural cane sugar

30 g/¼ cup whole blanched almonds

vanilla ice cream, to serve

for the almond slump batter:

200 g/1½ cups plain/all-purpose flour

3 teaspoons baking powder

a pinch of salt

100 g/1 cup ground almonds

about 350 ml/scant 1½ cups milk

4 tablespoons unsalted butter, melted

a large, non-stick baking pan

serves 4–6

This is a homely dish, easy to make and even easier to eat. Pears make a nice change from apples, which are more commonly used in rustic home-baked desserts. If you prefer to use apples, choose a tart green apple and replace the grated orange zest with lemon.

pear slump

900 g/2 lbs. pears, peeled, cored and sliced
75 g/½ cup light soft brown sugar
2 tablespoons plain/all-purpose flour
1 teaspoon vanilla extract
finely grated zest of 1 orange
vanilla ice cream or whipped cream, to serve

for the slump batter:

300 g/2 cups plain/all-purpose flour
200 g/1 cup caster/granulated sugar
1 tablespoon baking powder
a pinch of salt
250 ml/1 cup milk
125 g/1 stick plus 1 tablespoon unsalted butter, melted
extra sugar or cinnamon sugar, to sprinkle

a large, shallow ovenproof dish, well-buttered

serves 4–6

Preheat the oven to 190°C (375°F) Gas 5.

In a bowl, combine the pears, sugar, flour, vanilla extract and orange zest. Toss gently with your hands to combine and arrange in an even layer in the bottom of the prepared baking dish. Set aside.

To prepare the slump batter, combine the flour, sugar, baking powder and salt in a separate bowl. In a third bowl or jug/pitcher, stir together the milk and melted butter. Gradually pour the milk mixture into the dry ingredients, beating with a wooden spoon until just smooth.

Drop spoonfuls of the batter on top of the pears, leaving gaps but spreading to the edges. Sprinkle the top with sugar and bake in the preheated oven for 40–50 minutes, until golden brown. Serve warm with vanilla ice cream or whipped cream.

Granny Smith apples were first cultivated in Australia by Maria Ann Smith who saw their potential as a good all-round cooking apple. Their flesh collapses when cooked so they work well in this self-saucing pudding. Blueberries are used here but if you see mulberries (which are seasonal and rarely grown commercially), don't hesitate to use them in this recipe.

Granny Smith & blueberry pudding

Preheat the oven to 180°C (350°F) Gas 4.

Peel and core the apples then thinly slice them directly into the prepared baking dish, arranging them in the bottom of the dish with the blueberries.

Sift the flour, baking powder and caster/granulated sugar into a large bowl. Put the buttermilk and egg in a separate bowl. Use the tip of a small sharp knife to scrape the seeds from the vanilla bean directly into the buttermilk mixture. Pour this mixture into the flour mixture and beat well to combine.

Pour the batter over the fruit in the baking dish. Working quickly, put the soft brown sugar in a jug/pitcher and add 250 ml/1 cup of boiling water. Stir until the sugar has dissolved. Carefully pour this mixture into the baking dish, pouring into a corner.

Bake in the preheated oven for 45 minutes, until the surface feels dry and springs back when lightly touched. Serve warm with cream.

2 tart green apples, such as Granny Smith

150 g/1 cup blueberries

125 g/1 cup plain/all-purpose flour

3 teaspoons baking powder

115 g/½ cup plus 2 tablespoons caster/granulated sugar

250 ml/1 cup buttermilk

1 egg

1 vanilla bean, split lengthways

100 g/½ cup soft light brown sugar

chilled single/light cream, to serve

a large ovenproof dish, well buttered

serves 6

These soft, pear-shaped fruits have a sweet, honey-nectar flavour. Once picked, they ripen very quickly and late-season figs are perfect baked in desserts. This indulgent recipe is an excellent way to use up leftover stale croissants and can be put together in no time at all.

fig & honey croissant pudding

2 croissants, preferably stale, each torn into 6 pieces
6 figs, halved
60 ml/¼ cup honey
3 eggs
250 ml/1 cup milk
250 ml/1 cup single/light cream
55 g/¼ cup caster/granulated sugar
chilled double/heavy cream, to serve

a medium ovenproof dish, lightly buttered

serves 4

Preheat the oven to 180°C (350°F) Gas 4.

Put the croissant pieces in the bottom of the prepared baking dish. Arrange the fig halves in between the croissant pieces and drizzle the honey over the top.

Combine the eggs, milk, cream and sugar in a bowl and pour into the dish. Let sit for about 20 minutes to allow the croissants to absorb some of the liquid. Bake in the preheated oven for about 50 minutes, until the top of the pudding is a dark golden brown.

Let cool slightly before serving with cream.

This is a very impressive dessert for relatively little work. The sweet and buttery brioche works well with the tangy blackberries. Try and find very sweet blackberries for this, as they will be softer and juicier, which is exactly what you want here. The dark purple juices should bleed into the brioche to create a pretty, marbled effect.

brioche pudding with blackberries

Preheat the oven to 180°C (350°F) Gas 4.

Slice the brioche to give you 6–8 thin slices. Lightly butter the slices on one side and arrange half of them in the bottom of a baking dish, overlapping them slightly. Arrange half of the blackberries on top. Repeat with the remaining brioche slices and blackberries.

Put the cream, eggs, milk and caster/granulated sugar in a bowl or jug/pitcher and beat to combine. Pour the mixture over the brioche in the baking dish. Cover with foil and let sit for 30 minutes to allow the brioche to absorb some of the liquid.

Sprinkle the demerara sugar over the top of the pudding and bake in the preheated oven for 40–45 minutes, until golden brown. Serve warm with vanilla ice cream.

4 brioche rolls (or half a 400-g/14-oz. brioche loaf)

50 g/½ cup unsalted butter, softened

300 g/2 cups blackberries

3 eggs

125 ml/½ cup single/light cream

375 ml/1½ cups milk

75 g/⅓ cup caster/granulated sugar

2 tablespoons demerara sugar

vanilla ice cream, to serve

a medium ovenproof dish

serves 6

This delightfully fresh-tasting dessert is based on a traditional British recipe. Served warm, the bottom layer forms a tangy, lemon sauce for the light sponge layer, but it is also delicious cold, when the sauce sets into a light custard that is lovely with the taste of blackberries. So there you are – two recipes for the price of one!

lemon & blackberry puddings

200–250 g/1½ cups ripe blackberries

100 g/½ cup caster/granulated sugar, plus 1 tablespoon

4 tablespoons unsalted butter, softened

1 vanilla bean, split lengthways

grated zest and freshly squeezed juice of 1 large lemon

2 large eggs, separated

2 slightly generous tablespoons plain/all-purpose flour

250 ml/1 cup milk

4 tablespoons single/light cream

½ teaspoon cream of tartar

chilled single/light cream, to serve

4–5 small ovenproof dishes, buttered

serves 4–5

Preheat the oven to 180°C (350°F) Gas 4.

Put the blackberries and the 1 tablespoon sugar in a bowl, toss gently, then spoon into the prepared baking dishes.

Put the butter and the remaining sugar in a bowl and beat until creamy. Use the tip of a small sharp knife to scrape the vanilla seeds directly into the mixture and beat to mix. Beat in the lemon zest, followed by the egg yolks. Sift in the flour, stir in, then gradually beat in the milk, cream and lemon juice.

Put the egg whites and cream of tartar in a separate, grease-free bowl and whisk until stiff but not dry. Beat 2 tablespoons of the egg whites into the pudding mixture, then fold in the remainder with a spatula. Spoon the mixture into the baking dishes. Put the dishes on a baking sheet and bake in the preheated oven for 30–35 minutes, until the sponge is golden. Serve hot or warm, with cream.

Variation To serve cold, bake in a 1-litre/4-cup shallow ovenproof dish for an additional 5–10 minutes. Let cool (it will sink and deflate), then chill. When ready to serve, whisk 200 ml/¾ cup whipping cream and 2 tablespoons vanilla sugar in a bowl until billowy and thick. Spread the cream over the pudding, then decorate with extra blackberries and strips of lemon zest.

There is nothing better on a cold winter's day than the sound of a steamed pudding gently rattling in its pan. Smaller oranges are best here, and don't peel them – they are cooked, skins and all, for maximum effect. The dates keep the dark, sticky sponge beautifully moist.

chocolate, orange & date steamed pudding

2–3 seedless oranges, unpeeled and each one cut into 6 neat slices

150 ml/⅔ cup sugar syrup*

200 g/1¾ sticks unsalted butter, softened

200 g/1 cup dark muscovado sugar

finely grated zest of 1 unwaxed orange

3 tablespoons fine-cut orange marmalade

3 eggs, beaten

1 tablespoon orange flower water (optional)

150 g/1 cup plus 2 tablespoons plain/all-purpose flour

50 g/6 tablespoons unsweetened cocoa powder

2 teaspoons baking powder

150 g/1 cup ready-to-eat stoned/pitted dates, chopped

hot custard, to serve

a 1.2-litre/6-cup pudding basin, buttered and base-lined with a disc of non-stick baking parchment

serves 6–8

Submerge the orange slices in the sugar syrup. Set a disc of non-stick baking parchment on top and simmer gently for 30–40 minutes. Lift the oranges out with a slotted spoon and drain on a wire rack. Boil the syrup hard until reduced by half and set aside. Place the best orange slice on top of the paper disc in the pudding basin. Use the rest of the slices to line the sides.

In a large bowl, cream the butter, muscovado sugar and orange zest, until light and fluffy. Beat in the marmalade, then gradually beat in the eggs and orange flower water, if using, mixing very well between each addition. Sift the flour, cocoa and baking powder onto a sheet of baking parchment, then tip into the egg mixture and fold in. Finally, fold in the dates.

Spoon the mixture into the orange-lined basin. Level the surface and cover with a disc of non-stick baking parchment. Take a large sheet of foil and fold it in half. Make a pleat in the centre and place over the basin, with the pleat in the centre. Press the foil over the side of the basin, tie around the top with string and trim away any excess foil. Stand the basin on a trivet in a large, deep saucepan and add enough water to come at least 5 cm/2 inches up the sides. Cover the pan with a lid and simmer gently for 2 hours, topping up the water level from time to time.

Remove the foil and paper disc and insert a skewer into the centre of the pudding – if it doesn't come out clean, re-cover and steam for a little longer. Loosen the pudding around the sides with a thin-bladed knife, turn out onto a plate and brush with some of the reserved sugar syrup. Serve hot with custard.

* To make a sugar syrup, pour 150 ml/⅔ cup water into a small saucepan and add 100 g/½ cup golden caster/natural cane sugar. Cook over gentle heat until dissolved.

pies, tarts & strudels

There are several different ways to top this alternative to a classic apple pie, including a lattice crust or this streusel topping, which is not strictly speaking Dutch as it comes from the Amish communities of America.

Dutch apple pie

500 g/1 lb. 2 oz. ready-made shortcrust pastry, thawed if frozen

1.3 kg/3 lbs. tart eating apples, such as Cox's, Jonagold or Braeburn

100 g/½ cup sugar

100 g/¾ cup sultanas/golden raisins

1 teaspoon ground cinnamon

1 tablespoon freshly squeezed lemon juice

whipped cream, to serve

for the streusel topping:

90 g/½ cup light soft brown sugar

45 g/½ cup less 2 tablespoons plain/all-purpose flour

120 g/1 stick unsalted butter, chilled

1 teaspoon ground cinnamon

1 teaspoon ground nutmeg

1 teaspoon ground allspice

a pinch of salt

80 g/½ cup shelled walnuts, chopped

a springform cake pan, 24 cm/9½ inches diameter, buttered and floured

serves 6–8

Preheat the oven to 180°C (350°F) Gas 4.

Roll out the pastry on a floured work surface and line the cake pan with the pastry, all the way up the sides to the top edge. Refrigerate while you prepare the apples.

Peel, core and dice the apples and put them in a bowl. Add the sugar, sultanas/golden raisins, cinnamon and lemon juice and mix well using your hands.

In a food processor, combine all the topping ingredients, except the walnuts, and process to form coarse crumbs. Add the walnuts and pulse just a few times to combine.

Put the apple mixture in the pastry-lined pan. Sprinkle the streusel topping over the top in an even layer, going all the way to the edges and tidy up the edges of the pastry.

Cover with foil and bake in the preheated oven for about 30 minutes. Remove the foil and continue baking for a further 25–30 minutes, until the top of the pie is golden. Serve warm with whipped cream.

Apple pie afficionados believe that the best pies are made with a variety of apples to achieve a combination of sweet and tart flavours with both firm and melting textures.

classic apple pie

1.3 kg/3 lbs. mixed apples, such as Cox's, Jonagold, Braeburn and Golden Delicious, peeled and cored

50 g/¼ cup sugar, or more to taste

1 teaspoon ground cinnamon

1 tablespoon freshly squeezed lemon juice

chilled single/light cream, to serve

for the pie pastry:

300 g/2 cups plus 2 tablespoons plain/all-purpose flour

1 teaspoon sugar

¼ teaspoon salt

75 g/⅔ stick unsalted butter

75 g/⅔ stick lard or vegetable shortening

1 egg yolk

1 egg, beaten

sugar, for sprinkling

a pie dish or plate (with sloping sides), 23 cm/9 inches diameter, buttered

serves 6–8

To make the pastry, put the flour, sugar and salt in a food processor and process just to combine. Add the butter and lard and process using the pulse button until the mixture just forms coarse crumbs. Add the egg yolk and 4 tablespoons cold water and pulse again; the mixture should be crumbly but not holding together.

Transfer to a floured work surface and form into a ball. Cut in half, wrap well in clingfilm/plastic wrap and chill for at least 1 hour. Roll out one dough half and use to line the bottom of the pie dish. Trim the edges leaving a 1 cm/½ inch overhang and save the pastry trimmings for decoration. Chill while you prepare the apples.

Cut the apples into slices; not too thick and not too thin. Put them in a bowl with the sugar, cinnamon and lemon juice and use your hands to mix well. Transfer to the lined pie dish.

Preheat the oven to 190°C (375°F) Gas 5.

Roll out the remaining dough on a floured work surface to a circle large enough to cover the pie dish. Brush the edges of the dough in the dish with beaten egg, then lay the other pastry circle on top. Fold over the overhang from the bottom layer and crimp using your fingertips, or use the tines of a fork to seal. Decorate as desired (a few leaves are traditional) and brush lightly with egg, then sprinkle with sugar. Cut 6–8 small slits in the top of the pie.

Put on a baking sheet and bake in the preheated oven for about 50–60 minutes, until golden. Serve warm with cream.

This twist on a classic recipe has a spice-filled pastry which takes on a golden colour. Rolling out the rustic and crumbly pastry and filling it with lemon-infused apples is a very relaxing process you will want to enjoy again and again.

dusky apple pie

8 tart green eating apples (such as Granny Smith), peeled, cored and thinly sliced

2 teaspoons freshly squeezed lemon juice

2 thin slices of lemon zest

55 g/¼ cup caster/granulated sugar

250 g/2 cups self-raising flour

185 g/¾ cup light soft brown sugar

1 tablespoon ground cinnamon

1 tablespoon ground ginger

125 g/1 stick plus 1 tablespoon unsalted butter, chilled and cubed

1 egg, lightly beaten

vanilla ice cream, to serve

a 20-cm/8-inch loose-based fluted tart pan, 4 cm/1½ inches high, lightly greased

serves 8–10

Put the apple slices in a large saucepan with the lemon juice, lemon zest and caster/granulated sugar. Cover and cook over low heat for 15–20 minutes, turning the apples often so they soften and cook evenly. Set aside and let cool.

To make the pastry, put the flour, brown sugar and spices in a food processor and process for a few seconds to combine. With the motor running, add the butter several cubes at a time. Add the egg and 1–2 tablespoons of cold water and process until combined. The dough will look dry and crumbly. Transfer to a bowl and knead to form a ball. Wrap the ball in clingfilm/plastic wrap and refrigerate for 30 minutes.

Preheat the oven to 180°C (350°F) Gas 4 and put a baking sheet in the oven to heat up.

Cut the dough into two portions, with one slightly larger than the other. Roll out the larger piece of dough between two sheets of baking parchment and use it to line the bottom and sides of the prepared tart pan. Take care when handling the pastry as it will be quite crumbly.

Spoon the apples on top of the pastry base. Roll out the remaining pastry to a circle large enough to cover the base and place on top of the pie, trimming the edges to fit. Use a small sharp knife to make several slits in the pastry. Put the pie on the hot baking sheet and bake in the preheated oven for 50–55 minutes, until the pastry is golden brown.

Remove the pie from the oven and let sit for 15–20 minutes before cutting into wedges and serving with vanilla ice cream.

The method of using layers of buttered filo/phyllo pastry and inverting the pie was inspired by the savoury Moroccan pie 'bastilla', but here the filling is vanilla-infused apples.

Moroccan apple pie

6 tart green eating apples, peeled, cored and thinly sliced

1 teaspoon finely grated lemon zest

2 tablespoons freshly squeezed lemon juice

1 vanilla bean, split lengthways

115 g/½ cup plus 2 tablespoons caster/granulated sugar

1 teaspoon ground cinnamon

1 teaspoon cornflour/cornstarch

80 g/¾ stick unsalted butter, melted and cooled

8 sheets of filo/phyllo pastry, thawed if frozen

icing/confectioners' sugar, for dusting

chilled single/light cream, to serve

a springform cake pan, 22 cm/9 inches diameter, lined with baking parchment

serves 8–10

Put the apples in a bowl with the lemon zest and juice. Use the tip of a small sharp knife to scrape the vanilla seeds directly into the bowl with the apples. Add half of the caster/granulated sugar and toss to coat. Put the remaining sugar in a small bowl with the cinnamon and mix to combine. Set aside.

Put the apples in a saucepan with 2 tablespoons water and set over medium heat. Cover and cook for 10 minutes, stirring occasionally, until the apples are soft. Transfer the apples to a bowl and let cool. When completely cool, stir in the cornflour/cornstarch.

Preheat the oven to 220°C (425°F) Gas 7. Put a baking sheet in the oven to heat. Brush the cake pan with melted butter.

Lay a sheet of filo/phyllo on a clean work surface and lightly brush with melted butter. Sprinkle over some of the cinnamon sugar. Repeat using 3 more sheets of filo/phyllo. Lift the filo/phyllo into the cake pan. Gently press it into the pan, letting the ends hang over the rim. Repeat with the remaining filo/phyllo, but lay the second stack across the first one so that the entire rim of the pan is draped in pastry. Spoon the apples into the pan and use the back of a spoon to gently press them down. Fold the ends of the filo/phyllo towards the centre of the pan to enclose the filling. Lightly brush with melted butter.

Working quickly, remove the hot baking sheet from the oven and line with baking parchment. Carefully invert the pan onto the sheet. Remove the side and base of the pan and brush the top of the pie with melted butter. Bake in the preheated oven for 30–35 minutes, until golden and crisp. Dust liberally with icing/confectioners' sugar and serve warm with cream.

This appealingly sticky, fruity tart tastes better the day after it's made. Freezing the raspberries beforehand ensures that they keep their shape during baking and don't become too mushy.

raspberry & almond tart

Preheat the oven to 180°C (350°F) Gas 4.

To make the pastry, put the ground almonds, flour and sugar in a food processor. With the motor running, add a cube of butter at a time until it is all incorporated and the mixture resembles coarse breadcrumbs. Add 2 tablespoons cold water and process until just combined. Be careful not to overprocess.

Tip the pastry out onto a lightly floured work surface and knead to form a ball. Roll the pastry out between 2 layers of baking parchment until it is about 5 cm/2 inches longer and 5 cm/2 inches wider than the tart pan. Carefully lift the pastry into the pan and use your fingers to press it down into the base and sides, letting it overhang. Prick the base all over with a fork and bake in the preheated oven for 20 minutes, until lightly golden. Simply break off the overhanging pastry.

Put the egg, sugar and flour in a bowl and whisk until thick and pale. Put the butter in a small saucepan and set over medium heat. Let melt until frothy and dark golden with a nutty aroma. Working quickly, pour the melted butter over the egg mixture and beat well. Scatter the frozen raspberries in the tart case. Pour the warm batter over the raspberries. Bake in the still-hot oven for about 45 minutes, until the top resembles a golden meringue. Let cool for 30 minutes before serving. Cut into slices and serve with cream.

150 g/6 oz. fresh raspberries, frozen until firm

1 egg

3 tablespoons caster/granulated sugar

1 tablespoon plain/all-purpose flour

75 g/⅔ stick unsalted butter

chilled single/light cream, to serve

for the almond pastry:

50 g/⅓ cup ground almonds

200 g/1½ cups plain/all-purpose flour

80 g/generous ⅓ cup caster/granulated sugar

125 g/1 stick plus 1 tablespoon unsalted butter, chilled and cubed

a rectangular tart pan, about 37 x 10 cm/ 15 x 8 inches, lightly greased

serves 6–8

This deliciously easy recipe works best if the pears are on the overripe side so that they are fork-tender once cooked.

pear, almond & mascarpone tart

4 very ripe pears
1 tablespoon freshly squeezed lemon juice
4 tablespoons caster/granulated sugar, plus 2 tablespoons to sprinkle
125 g/½ cup mascarpone
1 egg
1 tablespoon plain/all-purpose flour
100 g/⅔ cup flaked/slivered almonds
chilled cream or vanilla ice cream, to serve

for the pastry:

200 g/1½ cups plain/all-purpose flour
4 tablespoons caster sugar
80 g/⅔ stick unsalted butter, chilled and cubed

a loose-bottomed tart pan, 24 cm/10 inches diameter, lightly greased and floured

serves 8–10

To make the pastry, put the flour and the 4 tablespoons sugar in a food processor and pulse to combine. With the motor running, add the butter and 1–2 tablespoons cold water and mix until the mixture resembles coarse breadcrumbs and starts to gather in lumps. Transfer to a lightly floured surface and briefly knead to form a ball. Wrap in clingfilm/plastic wrap and chill for 1 hour, until firm.

Preheat the oven to 180°C (350°F) Gas 4.

Coarsely grate the chilled pastry into a large bowl. Using lightly floured hands, scatter the grated pastry into the prepared tart pan and use your fingers to gently press it in, until the entire base and the side of the pan are covered. Bake in the preheated oven for about 25 minutes, until golden. Let cool.

Peel, halve and core the pears. Put them in a non-reactive bowl with the lemon juice and 1 tablespoon of the sugar. Put the remaining 3 tablespoons sugar in a food processor. Add the mascarpone, egg and flour and process to form a thick paste. Spread the mixture over the pastry. Arrange the pears on top and scatter with the almonds and sprinkling sugar. Bake in the still-hot oven for 40–45 minutes, until the pears are soft and the mascarpone mixture has set. Slice and serve with cream or vanilla ice cream.

These individual tarts are so simple and quick to make. Use Red Delicious apples in early autumn at a time when blueberries are in their last few weeks. Both fruits are perfect to cook with and lovely with vanilla. Any leftover tarts can be served cold the next day. Just dust them with some icing/confectioners' sugar and eat them as you would a fruit-filled Danish pastry.

apple & blueberry tarts

375-g/13-oz. sheet of ready-rolled puff pastry, thawed if frozen

2 tablespoons caster/granulated sugar

1 vanilla bean, split lengthways

3 sweet eating apples, such as Red Delicious or Braeburn, cored and cut into wedges

150 g/generous 1 cup blueberries

chilled double/heavy cream, to serve

a baking sheet lined with baking parchment

serves 4

Preheat the oven to 220°C (425°F) Gas 7.

Lightly flour a work surface and unroll the pastry. Flatten it out and use a sharp knife or a pizza wheel to cut it into 4 squares. Transfer the squares to the prepared baking sheet.

Put the sugar and 2 tablespoons of water in a saucepan and bring to the boil, stirring until the sugar dissolves. Use the tip of a small sharp knife to scrape the vanilla seeds directly into the sugar syrup and stir to combine.

Add the apple slices to the pan, reduce the heat to medium and cook for 4–5 minutes, turning the apples gently so they cook evenly. Add the blueberries and gently stir to coat them in the sweet syrup. Arrange the apples and blueberries on top of each pastry square. Bake in the preheated oven for 18–20 minutes, until the pastry is puffed and golden. Serve warm with the cream spooned over the top.

Variation For a simple French-style apple frangipane tart, mix 2 tablespoons each of room temperature butter, ground almonds and icing/confectioners' sugar with 1 tablespoon plain/all-purpose flour in a bowl until you have a paste. Stir in 1 egg yolk until smooth. Spread the mixture over each of the pastry squares, leaving a space around the edge, and top with the apple slices. Bake in a preheated oven at 220°C (425°F) Gas 7 for 18–20 minutes, until puffed and golden.

You can use practically any fruit here; small peaches, nectarines, apricots, plums, apples, blueberries, pineapple or a mixture of berries. Flaked almonds, walnuts and pecan nuts would also be good added to the fruits. To crush sugar cubes, put them in a plastic freezer bag and beat with the end of a rolling pin. Sprinkle over the tarts for a deliciously crunchy effect.

caramelized pear & cranberry tarts

375-g/13-oz. sheet of ready-rolled puff pastry, thawed if frozen

2 large ripe pears, peeled, halved and cored

25 g/1 oz. dried cranberries

25 g/2 tablespoons unsalted butter, chilled and cubed

milk, to glaze

3 tablespoons granulated sugar or 75 g/2½ oz. sugar cubes, crushed (see recipe introduction)

1 teaspoon ground cinnamon

chilled double/heavy cream or crème fraîche, to serve

serves 4

Preheat the oven to 220°C (425°F) Gas 7. Put a non-stick baking sheet in the oven to heat.

Lightly flour a work surface and unroll the pastry. Flatten it out and use a sharp knife or a pizza wheel to cut it into 4 squares.

Place a pear half in the centre of each pastry square and divide the dried cranberries between the squares. Scatter with the diced butter. Brush the edges with a little milk. Mix the granulated sugar or crushed sugar cubes with the cinnamon and sprinkle over the top.

Carefully slide the tarts onto the hot baking sheet and return to the preheated oven to cook for about 35–40 minutes, until the pastry is golden brown and crisp and the pears are tender. Serve warm with cream or crème fraîche.

Which apple variety to use for a tarte tatin is the source of much debate. Golden Delicious are good because they hold their shape well and the mild flavour complements the rich caramel.

tarte tatin

150 g/1 stick plus 2 tablespoons unsalted butter

150 g/¾ cup caster/granulated sugar

1.5 kg/3 lbs. 5 oz. tart eating apples, such as Golden Delicious or Cox's, peeled, cored and quartered

crème fraîche, to serve

for the sweet pastry dough:

200 g/1½ cups plain/all-purpose flour

2 teaspoons caster sugar

100 g/1 stick unsalted butter, chilled and cubed

a heavy, flameproof tarte tatin pan (ideally enamelled cast iron or lined copper), 20 cm/8 inches diameter

serves 6

To make the pastry, put the flour, sugar, butter and salt in a food processor and using the pulse button, process until the mixture is just combined (about 5–10 pulses). Add 3–4 tablespoons cold water and pulse just until the dough holds together. Wrap the dough in baking parchment and let stand in a cool place for 30–60 minutes before rolling out.

Roll out the pastry on a floured work surface. Turn the tart pan upside-down on the rolled out dough and trace around it with the tip of a sharp knife. Transfer to a large plate and chill.

Put the butter and sugar in the tart pan and set over high heat. Melt, stirring to blend. Remove from the heat and arrange the apple quarters in the pan in 2 circles. (The inner circle should go in the opposite direction to the outer circle.) Return to the heat and cook for about 30 minutes. From this point, watch the apples carefully and cook for a further 5–15 minutes, until the liquid thickens and caramelizes.

Preheat the oven to 200°C (400°F) Gas 6. Remove the pan from the heat and top with the pastry round, gently tucking in the edges. Transfer to the preheated oven and bake for about 45 minutes, until browned. Let cool only slightly. Carefully invert the tart onto a serving plate so that the pastry is on the bottom. Serve at room temperature with crème fraîche.

What could be better than the simplicity of pears poached in red wine? This tart is! The fruit absorbs the deep flavour of the wine and turns a fabulously rich colour. If you want to be outrageously extravagant, use Italian Vin Santo or Marsala instead of wine and reduce the quantity of sugar – the pears will be a beautiful dark mahogany.

drunken pear tart

8 under-ripe medium pears

1 cinnamon stick

75 g/⅓ cup caster sugar

600 ml/2⅓ cups full-bodied red wine

chopped pistachios or flaked/slivered almonds, to finish

crème fraîche, to serve

for the pâte brisée:

200 g/1½ cups plain/all-purpose flour

a large pinch of salt

100 g/1 stick unsalted butter, diced, at room temperature

1 egg yolk

2½–3 tablespoons iced water

a cast-iron frying pan/skillet, 25 cm/10 inches diameter

serves 6

To make the pastry, sift the flour and salt into a mound on a clean work surface. Make a well in the centre with your fist. Put the butter and egg yolk into the well and using the fingers of one hand 'peck' the eggs and butter together until they resemble scrambled eggs. Using a palette knife, flick the flour over the egg mixture and chop through until almost amalgamated. Sprinkle with the iced water and chop again. Bring together quickly with your hands. Knead lightly into a ball, then flatten slightly. Wrap in clingfilm/plastic wrap and chill for at least 30 minutes. Let return to room temperature before rolling out.

Peel the pears, halve lengthways and carefully scoop out the core with a teaspoon or melon baller. Arrange them around the base of the frying pan in concentric circles. Crumble the cinnamon over the top and sprinkle with the sugar. Pour in the red wine, bring to the boil, then cover and simmer gently for about 1 hour, until tender.

Preheat the oven to 200°C (400°F) Gas 6. Uncover the pan and hold the pan lid over the pears to hold them back while you pour off the juices into a saucepan. Boil the juices until well reduced and syrupy, then pour back over the pears.

Roll out the dough on a lightly floured work surface to a circle slightly larger than the pan. Lift the pastry over the pears and tuck the edge of the pastry down into the pan. Bake for 35–40 minutes, until the pastry is crisp and golden. As soon as it is ready, invert the tart onto a plate, sprinkle with nuts and serve warm with crème fraîche.

Versions of this tart are sold at pâtisseries all over France. When peaches are in season and at their best, they appear in the window in all their rustic glory. So simple to make and so good to eat! If you want to use ready-made puff pastry, that's fine, but you should try this easy cheat's recipe at least once.

free-form peach tart

4–6 ripe peaches
55 g/½ stick butter
freshly squeezed juice of ½ a lemon
150 g/¾ cup caster/granulated sugar
whipped cream or crème fraîche, to serve

for the cheat's puff pastry:

250 g/2 cups plain/all-purpose flour
a pinch of salt
150 g/1¼ sticks unsalted butter, frozen
about 150 ml/½ cup iced water

a dinner plate, about 28 cm/11 inches diameter (to use as a template)

serves 6

To make the pastry, sift the flour and salt into a large bowl. Hold the frozen butter in a clean dish towel and, using the large side of a box grater, quickly grate the butter into the flour. Stir the butter into the flour with a palette knife until it is evenly distributed. Sprinkle the water over the surface, then mix with the knife until the dough starts to come together in a messy lump. Tip this onto a floured work surface and knead lightly until it forms a streaky, lumpy ball. Flatten the ball with the palm of your hand. Wrap in clingfilm/plastic wrap and chill for 30 minutes until firm. Unwrap and roll out away from you into a rectangle 3 times longer than it is wide – no exact measurements are needed here but it should be about 1 cm/½ inch thick. Lightly mark the pastry into 3 equal sections with a blunt knife. Fold the third closest to you up over the middle third, then bring the top third towards you over the folded two-thirds. Rewrap and chill for 15 minutes. Repeat twice more. Wrap and chill for 30 minutes.

Preheat the oven to 230°C (450°F) Gas 8. Roll out the pastry on a lightly floured work surface and cut out a circle using a large dinner plate as a template. Lift onto a baking sheet and make an edge by twisting the pastry over itself all the way around the edge. Press lightly to seal. Still on the baking sheet, chill or freeze for 30 minutes.

Peel the peaches, then halve and stone/pit them and cut into chunky slices. Put the butter into a large saucepan, then add the lemon juice and half the sugar. Heat until melted, then add the peaches and toss gently. Pile the peaches over the pastry. Sprinkle with the remaining sugar and bake in the preheated oven for 20–25 minutes, until golden, puffed and caramelized. Serve with whipped cream or crème fraîche.

These unusual tartlets are a cheese course and dessert rolled into one making them a fabulous finale for any dinner party.

pear, gorgonzola & pecan tartlets

375-g/13-oz. sheet of ready-rolled puff pastry, thawed if frozen
1 egg, lightly beaten
200 g/7 oz. Gorgonzola
4 tablespoons double/heavy cream
2–3 ripe pears
75 g/½ cup pecan halves
6 teaspoons pure maple syrup
cayenne pepper, to taste

serves 6

Preheat the oven to 220°C (425°F) Gas 7.

Unroll the pastry, cut it in half horizontally, then cut each of the halves into 3 to make 6 equal-sized pieces. With the tip of a sharp knife, score round each of the squares about 1.5 cm/ ½ inch from the edge to make a border. Lightly brush the border with beaten egg, taking care not to brush over the cut you've made (otherwise the pastry won't puff up around the edge of the tartlets).

Put the Gorgonzola in a bowl and break up roughly with a fork, then stir in the cream. Season with a little cayenne pepper and spread over the bases of the tartlets, taking care not to cover the border. Roughly break up the pecan nuts and divide between the tartlets. Peel, core and quarter the pears, cut each quarter into 3 wedges and lay them in slices on top of the cheese and nuts. Drizzle a teaspoonful of maple syrup over each tart and bake in the preheated oven for 15–20 minutes, until the pastry is well browned and puffed up. Let cool for 5 minutes before serving.

Apple tart is a classic but this recipe represents a slight departure. The combination of apples and vanilla is absolutely divine so a layer of vanilla-scented apple purée has been added.

apple tart

Roll out the pastry dough on a floured work surface to a circle slightly larger than the prepared tart pan. Transfer the dough to the pan. To trim the edges, roll a rolling pin over the top, using the edge of the pan as a cutting surface, letting the excess pastry fall away. Refrigerate for 30 minutes, until firm.

To bake blind, preheat the oven to 200°C (400°F) Gas 6. Prick the pastry base all over, line with baking parchment and fill with baking beans. Bake in the preheated oven for 15 minutes, then remove the paper and beans and bake for a further 10–15 minutes, until golden. Let cool before filling.

To make the apple and vanilla purée, put the apples, vanilla bean, sugar and butter in a saucepan with 3–4 tablespoons water. Cook gently, stirring often, for about 10–15 minutes until soft (adding more water if necessary). Remove the vanilla bean, use the tip of a small sharp knife to scrape the vanilla seeds directly into the mixture, then discard the bean. Transfer the mixture to a food processor and purée until smooth.

Preheat the oven to 190°C (375°F) Gas 5. Spread the purée evenly in the pastry case. Arrange the apple slices in a neat circle around the edge; they should be slightly overlapping. Repeat to create an inner circle, trimming the slices slightly so that they fit, going in the opposite direction from the outer circle. Brush with melted butter and sprinkle over the sugar.

Bake in the preheated oven for 25–25 minutes, until the apples are just browned and tender. Serve warm with cream.

1 quantity Sweet Pastry Dough (see page 117), at room temperature

3 mild eating apples, such as Golden Delicious, peeled, cored and sliced

1 tablespoon unsalted butter, melted

1 tablespoon sugar

chilled single/light cream, to serve

For the apple and vanilla purée

3 apples (any variety), peeled, cored and diced

1 vanilla bean, split lengthways

2–4 tablespoons caster/granulated sugar, to taste

2 teaspoons unsalted butter

a loose-based tart pan, 27 cm/11 inches diameter, buttered and lightly floured

serves 6–8

This is a classic French pastry. Sometimes the pears are simply halved, but it looks more attractive if they are sliced.

pear & almond tart

1 part-baked sweet pastry case, 27 cm/11 inch diameter or 35 x 11 cm/14 inch x 4½ inches, as shown (see Sweet Pastry Dough, page 117 and baking blind method, page 125)

100 g/1 stick unsalted butter, softened

100 g/½ cup caster/granulated sugar

2 large eggs

100 g/⅔ cup ground almonds

2 tablespoons plain/all-purpose flour

seeds from ½ a vanilla bean split lengthways, or 1 teaspoon vanilla extract

3–4 ripe pears, such as Williams, peeled, cored and sliced

vanilla ice cream or hot custard, to serve

serves 6

Preheat the oven to 190°C (375°F) Gas 5.

In a mixing bowl, combine the butter and sugar and beat until light and fluffy. Add the eggs one at a time, beating well with each addition. Add the almonds, flour and vanilla seeds and mix just to combine.

Spoon the almond mixture into the pastry case and level the surface. Arrange the pear slices on top.

Bake in the preheated oven for 20–25 minutes, until puffed and golden. Serve warm with vanilla ice cream or custard.

Fresh ricotta cheese is combined here with summer-ripe cherries and crispy filo/phyllo pastry with great success. Best of all, you can make this in advance and freeze it. There is no need to thaw before cooking – just give it a little more time in the oven. You could try using sliced green apples instead of the cherries.

cherry & ricotta strudel

500 g/1 lb. fresh cherries, stoned/pitted and halved

60 g/⅓ cup icing/confectioners' sugar, plus extra for dusting

2 teaspoons cornflour/cornstarch

8 sheets of filo/phyllo pastry, thawed if frozen

100 g/⅔ cup ground almonds

150 g/6 oz. fresh ricotta

75 g/¾ stick unsalted butter, melted

serves 8

Put the cherries, 1 tablespoon of the icing/confectioners' sugar and the cornflour/cornstarch in a bowl and let sit for 30 minutes, stirring often.

Preheat the oven to 220°C (425°F) Gas 7. Put a baking sheet in the oven to heat up.

Put the ground almonds and 2 tablespoons of the remaining icing/confectioners' sugar in a bowl and mix to combine. Put the ricotta in a separate bowl, add the remaining icing/confectioners' sugar and mix to combine. Set aside.

Put a sheet of baking parchment on a work surface. Lay a sheet of filo/phyllo on the baking parchment, longest edge nearest to you. Brush all over with melted butter until the filo/phyllo is shiny. Sprinkle 1–2 tablespoons of the ground almond mixture over the pastry. Repeat with the remaining sheets of filo/phyllo, melted butter and almond mixture, finishing with the final sheet of filo/phyllo.

Working quickly, so that the filo/phyllo does not become soggy, spread the ricotta mixture over the pastry, leaving a 5-cm/2-inch margin around the edges. Spoon the cherry mixture over the top. Fold the edge nearest to you up and over the filling, tucking in the shorter edges as you roll. Make sure the strudel is sitting seam-side down. Use the baking parchment to lift the strudel onto the hot baking sheet. Bake in the preheated oven for 12–15 minutes, until lightly golden brown.

Remove and let cool slightly before dusting liberally with icing/confectioners' sugar and cutting into slices to serve.

Praline powder is a great 'secret' ingredient. It's a cinch to prepare and makes a great addition to many desserts. Here it teams up with flaky filo/phyllo pastry to lift what would be an ordinary strudel well above the average.

praline apple strudel

450 g/1 lb. tart eating apples, such as Cox's or Braeburn, peeled, cored and chopped

75 g/¼ cup mixed dried fruit, such as sultanas/golden raisins, cranberries or sour cherries

100 g/½ cup light brown sugar

1 teaspoon ground cinnamon

1 tablespoon unsalted butter

6 sheets filo/phyllo pastry, thawed if frozen

50 g/½ stick unsalted butter, melted

icing/confectioners' sugar, to dust

whipped cream or crème fraîche, to serve

for the praline:

75 g/½ cup pecan halves

40 g/¼ cup caster/granulated sugar

a baking sheet lined with baking parchment

serves 6–8

To make the praline, combine the pecans and sugar in a non-stick heavy-based frying pan and cook over medium/high heat, stirring constantly, until the sugar hardens and coats the nuts. Transfer to a plate to cool, then process in a coffee grinder or small food processor until ground to a coarse powder. Set aside.

In a large saucepan, combine the apples, dried fruit, brown sugar, cinnamon and 1 tablespoon butter. Cook over medium heat for about 15 minutes, until the apples are soft and the juices have evaporated. Remove from the heat and let cool.

Preheat the oven to 190°C (375°F) Gas 5.

Put 2 sheets of filo/phyllo on the prepared baking sheet and brush with some melted butter. Sprinkle with a little praline. Top with 2 more sheets of filo/phyllo and repeat. Top with 2 more sheets of filo/phyllo. Spread the apple mixture in an even layer over the top sheet of pastry. Sprinkle with more praline mixture, then carefully roll up from a long end, as you would a Swiss/jelly roll. Use the baking parchment to help you roll, if necessary. Make sure the strudel is sitting seam-side down. Brush with a little more melted butter, sprinkle with any remaining praline and bake in the preheated oven for 25–35 minutes, until crisp and golden.

Let cool slightly before dusting with icing/confectioners' sugar. Serve warm with whipped cream or crème fraîche.

This simple recipe can be made with whatever fruit was in season, such as apples, pears or apricots – but plums are probably the nicest. How you shape the pastries depends upon the way the puff pastry dough is packaged: squares, circles and triangles all work fine. Be sure to use just-soft plums, not too ripe.

baked plums in puff pastry

375-g/13-oz. sheet of ready-rolled puff pastry, thawed if frozen

1 egg, beaten

50 g/¼ cup sugar, plus about 4 tablespoons caster/granulated sugar for sprinkling

6–8 large red plums (not too ripe)

200 g/scant 1 cup crème fraîche, sweetened with 1–2 tablespoons sugar

a baking sheet lined with baking parchment

serves 4

Preheat the oven to 190°C (375°F) Gas 5.

Roll out the pastry on a floured surface to make 4 rectangles, each about 15 x 9 cm/6 x 3½ inches. Arrange the pastry squares on the prepared baking sheet. Brush with the egg and use the 4 tablespoons caster/granulated sugar to sprinkle each rectangle very generously. Bake in the preheated oven for 15–20 minutes, until puffed and browned. Remove from the oven and let cool. Do not turn the oven off.

Cut the plums in half, remove the stones/pits, then slice each half into quarters. Put the plums in a baking dish, sprinkle with the sugar and bake in the still-hot oven for 20–30 minutes, until tender and slightly browned. Let cool.

To assemble, split the pastries in half with a sharp knife, but not all the way through. Fill with a generous dollop the sweetened crème fraîche and plums. Serve immediately, while the pastry is still crisp.

dessert cakes

Sweet summer strawberries are baked in a smooth, dense cake given a light and creamy crumb by using buttermilk. It can be made in a conventional round cake pan or baked in a square pan and cut into squares to serve (like a brownie). Small strawberries are fine left whole but do halve or quarter large ones before folding them through the batter.

strawberry buttermilk cake

250 g/2 cups self-raising flour

225 g/1 cup plus 2 tablespoons caster/granulated sugar

125 g/1 stick unsalted butter, softened

2 eggs

250 ml/1 cup buttermilk

375 g/13 oz. strawberries, hulled

hot custard or chilled double/heavy cream, to serve

for the topping:

40 g/5 tablespoons plain/all-purpose flour

50 g/½ stick unsalted butter, chilled and cubed

95 g/½ cup light soft brown sugar

a cake pan, 24-cm/9-inches square, greased and base-lined

serves 6–8

Preheat the oven to 180°C (350°F) Gas 4.

Put the flour and sugar in a bowl and stir to mix. Put the butter, eggs and buttermilk in the bowl of a food processor and process until smooth and combined. With the motor running, add the flour and sugar and process until well mixed. Scrape down the sides of the bowl to evenly incorporate all the ingredients. Transfer to a mixing bowl and stir in the strawberries. Spoon the mixture into the prepared cake pan and level the top.

To make the topping, put the flour and butter in a bowl and, using your fingertips, rub the butter into the flour until the mixture resembles coarse breadcrumbs. Stir in the sugar.

Sprinkle the topping mixture evenly over the cake mixture. Bake in the preheated oven for 50 minutes, until the top is golden brown.

Let cool before cutting into squares and serving with custard or cream.

Somewhere between an American shortcake and a scone, this cake has all the hallmarks of a great recipe – it's easy, delicious and has the 'I can't believe I made this myself' factor. Because the method is so simple the final result is largely dependent on the quality of the fruit used, so do choose the best peaches, still firm with that heady peach fragrance.

peach & raspberry scone cake

100 g/½ cup good-quality raspberry jam
250 ml/1 cup whipping cream, whipped
2 fresh peaches, stoned/pitted and sliced
300 g/2 cups fresh raspberries

for the scone cake:

375 g/2¾ cups self-raising flour
250 ml/1 cup whipping cream
250 ml/1 cup clear, sparkling lemonade (not low calorie or reduced sugar)

a fluted, loose-based tart pan, about 20 cm/8 inches diameter, lightly greased

serves 8

Preheat the oven to 180°C (350°F) Gas 4.

To make the scone cake, put the flour in a large bowl and make a well in the centre. Add the cream and lemonade and use a wooden spoon to mix together.

Spoon the mixture into the prepared pan, gently pressing down to fit. Bake in the preheated oven for 30–35 minutes, until golden brown on top. Let cool.

Using a long, sharp knife, slice about 0.5 cm/¼ inch off the top of the cake to create a level surface. Spread the jam evenly over the top of the cake.

Spoon the whipped cream on top of the cake, arrange the peaches slices and raspberries on top and serve immediately.

This is a deliciously spicy cake with a very moreish texture. Ground ginger loses its intensity if left sitting in the kitchen cupboard for too long, so do make sure that what you use here is not past it's use-by date. You can make this recipe substituting apples for the pears. If you do decide to try it this way, use ground cinnamon instead of ginger.

pear & ginger crumble cake

Preheat the oven to 180°C (350°F) Gas 4.

To make the crumble mixture, put the flour and ginger in a large bowl. Add the butter and quickly rub it into the flour using your fingertips. Add the sugar and rub again until the mixture resembles coarse sand. Refrigerate until needed.

Beat the butter and sugar until pale and creamy. Add the eggs, one at a time, and beat well between each addition. Tip in the flour and baking powder and beat for 1 minute, until the mixture is smooth and well combined. Pour it into the prepared cake pan. Toss the pears in a bowl with the lemon juice and put them on top of the cake. Sprinkle the crumble topping over the top. Bake in the preheated oven for 40–45 minutes, until golden on top.

Let cool slightly before removing from the pan and serve warm with cream.

125 g/1 stick unsalted butter, softened

125 g/½ cup plus 2 tablespoons caster/granulated sugar

2 eggs, at room temperature

125 g/1 cup plain/all-purpose flour

2 teaspoons baking powder

2 firm pears, peeled, cored and sliced

1 tablespoon freshly squeezed lemon juice

chilled double/heavy cream, to serve

for the ginger crumble:

60 g/½ cup plain/all-purpose flour

1 teaspoon ground ginger

3 tablespoons soft light brown sugar

50 g/½ stick unsalted butter, chilled and cubed

a springform cake pan, 20 cm/8 inches diameter, base-lined and lightly greased

You can use either yellow or white peaches here. Yellow peaches have a more robust flavour whereas the white ones have a more subtle flavour that is more like that of nectarines, which are, after all, peaches without the fuzzy skin!

upside-down peach cake

4 large fresh peaches
125 g/1 stick unsalted butter, softened
185 g/scant 1 cup light soft brown sugar
3 eggs, separated
185 g/¾ cup plus 2 tablespoons self-raising flour
250 ml/1 cup soured cream
icing/confectioners' sugar, for dusting
chilled single/light cream, to serve

a springform cake pan, 23 cm/9 inches diameter, base-lined and lightly greased

Preheat the oven to 180°C (350°F) Gas 4.

Halve the peaches, discard the stones/pits, then cut each into quarters. Arrange the peaches on the bottom of the prepared cake pan and set aside.

Put the butter and sugar in a large bowl and beat until the sugar has completely dissolved and the mixture is the colour of caramel. Add the egg yolks, one at a time, beating for 1 minute between each addition. Fold the flour and soured cream through in two batches.

In a separate grease-free bowl, beat the egg whites until they form firm peaks. Using a large metal spoon, fold the whites into the cake mixture in batches. Spoon the mixture over the peaches and level the surface. Bake in the preheated oven for 40–45 minutes, until the top of the cake is golden and the centre springs back when gently pressed.

Let cool for 10 minutes in the pan before carefully turning out. Dust with icing/confectioners' sugar and serve warm with cream.

This cake hails from Somerset, in England, but as traditional West Country cooking can be a little spartan, the basic recipe here has been jazzed up with some honey and spices.

spiced apple cake

Preheat the oven to 160°C (325°F) Gas 3.

Put the butter and brown sugar in a mixing bowl and cream together until light and fluffy. Beat in the honey. In a separate bowl, combine the flours, baking powder, cinnamon, cloves, ginger and nutmeg.

Fold the dry ingredients into the butter mixture, then add the eggs and mix well. Fold in the ground almonds, sultanas/golden raisins, apples and milk and mix just to combine. Transfer the mixture to the prepared pan and level the top.

Bake in the preheated oven for 50–60 minutes, until risen and golden and a skewer inserted in the centre of the cake comes out clean. Let cool slightly in the pan then turn out onto a wire rack. When cool, sprinkle with flaked/slivered almonds and dust with icing/confectioners' sugar. Cut into squares to serve.

225 g/2 sticks unsalted butter, softened

200 g/1 cup light soft brown sugar

6 tablespoons honey

275 g/2 cups wholemeal/whole-wheat flour

75 g/⅔ cup plain/all-purpose flour

2 teaspoons baking powder

1 teaspoon ground cinnamon

½ teaspoon ground cloves

½ teaspoon ground ginger

½ teaspoon ground nutmeg

5 eggs, beaten

3 tablespoons ground almonds

50 g/½ cup sultanas/golden raisins

550 g/1 lb. 4 oz. tart cooking apples, peeled, cored and finely chopped

4 tablespoons milk

3–4 tablespoons flaked/slivered almonds, toasted

icing/confectioners' sugar, for dusting

a cake pan, 23 cm/9 inches square, buttered and lightly floured

makes 16 squares

Use sweet eating apples here as they keep their shape, unlike cooking apples which can result in a wet and mushy cake. If you are using the standard size of ramekin this recipe will serve six, but if you have the larger ones it will serve four. The cakes can be cooked ahead of time, but leave them in the dishes and reheat in a warm oven before turning out and serving.

upside-down apple cakes

100 g/½ cup light soft brown sugar

175 g/1½ sticks unsalted butter, plus extra for greasing

350 g/12 oz. dessert apples, such as Braeburn or Cox's Orange Pippin, peeled, cored and roughly chopped

finely grated zest of ½ a lemon

½ teaspoon ground nutmeg

½ teaspoon ground cinnamon

25 g/1 oz. walnut halves

115 g/scant 1 cup self-raising flour

1 teaspoon baking powder

115 g/½ cup plus 1 tablespoon caster/granulated sugar

2 eggs

for the ginger cream:

4 tablespoons crème fraîche

2 pieces of stem ginger in syrup, drained and finely chopped

1 teaspoon of syrup from the stem ginger jar

6 x 150-ml/½-cup or 4 x 235-ml/1-cup ramekins, lightly greased

serves 4–6

Preheat the oven to 180°C (350°F) Gas 4.

Put the brown sugar and 60 g/4 tablespoons of the butter in a heavy-based saucepan with 2 tablespoons water and heat until melted. Gradually bring to the boil and cook for about 1 minute, or until caramelized. Spoon 1 tablespoon of the caramel sauce into the base of each prepared ramekin. Set aside the remaining sauce.

Put the apples, lemon zest, nutmeg, cinnamon and walnuts in a large bowl and mix to combine. Divide the mixture between the ramekins.

To make the sponge, put the remaining butter, flour, baking powder, and caster/granulated sugar in the bowl of a food processor and blend for a couple of seconds before adding the eggs. Process for a further 10–15 seconds, then stop as soon as the mixture comes together. Spoon the cake mixture into the ramekins. Place them on a baking sheet and cook in the preheated oven for 15–20 minutes, until the sponge bounces back when lightly touched.

Meanwhile, to make the ginger cream, mix together the crème fraîche, stem ginger and ginger syrup. Remove the cakes from the oven and run a knife around the edges. Leave to sit for about 5 minutes before inverting onto serving plates. To serve, reheat the reserved caramel sauce and spoon it over the cakes. Serve topped with a spoonful of the ginger cream.

If you can get hold of blood oranges, they are the best ones to use here. They have a sherberty flavour with hints of raspberry and a divine colour. The fact that they are a truly seasonal fruit, available only for a few months in the year, makes them even more special.

almond & orange syrup cake

250 g/1½ cups blanched almonds

225 g/1 cup plus 2 tablespoons caster/granulated sugar

50 g/6 tablespoons self-raising flour

250 g/2¼ sticks unsalted butter, softened

1 tablespoon finely grated orange zest

4 eggs

60 g/½ cup flaked/slivered almonds, lightly toasted

extra thick double/heavy cream, to serve

for the orange syrup:

65 ml/¼ cup freshly squeezed orange juice

55 g/¼ cup caster/granulated sugar

a springform cake pan, 22 cm/9 inches diameter, lightly greased

serves 8

Preheat the oven to 180°C (350°F) Gas 4.

Put the almonds in a food processor and process until finely chopped. Transfer to a bowl and mix in the sugar and flour.

Beat the butter and orange zest for 1 minute, then add the eggs, one at a time, beating well after each addition until well mixed. Add the almond mixture in two batches and beat again until well combined. Spoon into the prepared cake pan. Bake in the preheated oven for 45 minutes, until golden on top. Remove the cake from the oven and prick it all over with a toothpick or skewer.

To make the syrup, put the orange juice and sugar in a small saucepan and set over high heat. Stir until the sugar has dissolved. As soon as the mixture boils remove the pan from the heat and pour the syrup over the cake.

Let the cake cool in the pan then sprinkle the flaked/slivered almonds on top. Slice and serve with cream.

The whisked sponge method of cake making is popular in Italy and this recipe from Tuscany is very light in texture and studded with juicy chunks of apple. You can change the spice to cinnamon if you prefer but use a little more, as it is not as assertive as cloves. Italian cooks sometimes add finely chopped fresh rosemary to theirs, which makes it taste very special.

apple & lemon sponge cake

100 g/1 stick unsalted butter

4 sweet eating apples, such as Cox's Orange Pippin

finely grated zest of 2 lemons and the freshly squeezed juice of ½ a lemon

¼ teaspoon ground cloves

4 eggs

150 g/¾ cup caster/granulated sugar

150 g/¾ cup plain/all-purpose flour

1 teaspoon baking powder

a pinch of salt

3 tablespoons apricot jam, melted

a springform cake pan, 23 cm/9 inches diameter, well buttered and base-lined

serves 8

Melt the butter in a saucepan, then set aside to cool. Peel, core and cut the apples into medium chunks and put them in a bowl. Add the lemon zest, cloves and juice and toss to coat.

Put the eggs and sugar in a heatproof bowl and set it over a saucepan of simmering water. Whisk for about 15 minutes until glossy, thick and pale and doubled in volume. The mixture should hold a trail when the whisk is lifted out of the bowl. Remove the bowl from the heat and continue whisking for a further 5–10 minutes, until the mixture is cool.

Preheat the oven to 180°C (350°F) Gas 4.

Sift the flour, baking powder and salt together into a large bowl. Gently fold half the flour into the whisked mixture. Pour the cooled melted butter around the edge of the mixture and fold in. Fold in the remaining flour, then two-thirds of the apples. Be very careful when folding in – you want to keep as much air in the mixture as possible. Spoon the remaining apples into the base of the cake pan, then pour the cake mixture over the apples. Bake in the preheated oven for about 40 minutes, until risen, golden brown and firm when gently pressed in the centre.

Let cool in the pan for 5 minutes before inverting onto a wire rack to cool. Brush the top with the melted apricot jam just before serving.

There is a lovely retro charm, redolent of 1950s cookbooks, about making a sweet cake with a vegetable that's usually served savoury. Of course, the courgette/zucchini here performs the same function as grated carrot does in the more familiar carrot cake. It keeps this cake wonderfully fresh and moist.

lemon, courgette & poppyseed cake

Preheat the oven to 190°C (375°F) Gas 5.

Put the poppyseeds and lemon zest in a small bowl. Heat the milk until hot, stir it into the poppyseed mixture and let it cool while you make the cake mixture.

Cream the butter and sugar together until very light and fluffy. Beat in the egg yolks, one at a time, followed by the vanilla extract, flour and ground almonds. Fold in the grated courgettes/zucchini, followed by the poppyseed mixture. In a separate, grease-free bowl, whisk the eggs whites with the cream of tartar until stiff, then fold the egg whites into the cake mixture. Scrape the mixture into the prepared pan and level the surface.

Bake in the preheated oven for 50–60 minutes, until just firm to the touch and a skewer inserted into the centre comes out clean. Let the cake cool in the pan for 10 minutes before turning out onto a wire rack.

When cool, sift the icing/confectioners' sugar into a bowl, make a well in the centre and add the still-hot melted butter. Start to mix, adding enough lemon juice to make a spreadable frosting. Mix in the lemon zest, then spread over the cake. Leave for 1–2 hours to set before serving.

25 g/3 tablespoons poppyseeds

finely grated zest of 2 lemons

80 ml/⅓ cup milk

250 g/2¼ sticks unsalted butter, softened

280 g/1⅓ cups light soft brown sugar

4 large eggs, separated

½ teaspoon vanilla extract

200 g/1½ cups self-raising flour, sifted

80 g/⅔ cup ground almonds

250 g/9 oz. courgettes/zucchini, topped, tailed and coarsely grated

½ teaspoon cream of tartar

for the frosting:

220 g/1 cup icing/confectioners' sugar

25 g/2 tablespoons unsalted butter, melted

1 teaspoon finely grated lemon zest

2–3 tablespoons freshly squeezed lemon juice

a springform cake pan, 23 cm/9 inches diameter, buttered and base-lined

serves 8–10

Don't be tempted to use large figs here, as they will split and prevent the egg whites from cooking and the meringue will become sloppy. Instead look out for small, very black ones as they will work perfectly with the caramelly, golden meringue.

fresh fig & walnut meringue

150 g/1 cup walnut halves

8–10 small black fresh figs, halved

6 large egg whites

230 g/1¼ cups light soft brown sugar

a circle of baking parchment, 23 cm/9 inches diameter

serves 8–10

Preheat the oven to 180°C (350°F) Gas 4.

Put the walnuts on a baking sheet and toast in the preheated oven for 5 minutes, until just starting to turn golden. Remove and let cool. Do not turn off the oven.

Put the egg whites in a large, grease-free bowl and beat until they form soft peaks. Add one tablespoon of the sugar at a time, beating well between each addition, and continue until all the sugar has been added and the meringue is thick and fluffy and a caramel colour. Add the figs and walnuts and stir to combine.

Put the circle of baking parchment on a baking sheet. Use a large spoon to transfer the mixture onto the paper, keeping within the circle and using the back of the spoon to create dents and peaks.

Bake in the preheated oven for 40–45 minutes, until the peaks of the meringue are dark golden. Slide a large knife under the meringue to remove it from the paper and transfer it to a serving plate. Serve warm.

This recipe is really just an excuse to eat lots of fresh strawberries and cream. Don't feel pressured to make a 'perfect' meringue. This is supposed to be messy and something you want to eat, not something you are afraid to touch! It doesn't matter if the meringue splits or isn't crispy; it's not meant to be.

strawberry meringue roulade

3 egg whites

1 teaspoon cornflour/cornstarch

170 g/¾ cup caster/superfine sugar, plus 2 teaspoons

125 ml/½ cup whipping cream

3 tablespoons icing/confectioners' sugar, plus extra for dusting

250 g/2 cups strawberries, hulled and sliced

a baking sheet, lined with baking parchment and sprinkled with 1 teaspoon caster/superfine sugar

serves 4–6

Preheat the oven to 120°C (250°F) Gas ½.

Put the egg whites in a grease-free bowl, add the cornflour/cornstarch and beat until soft peaks form. Add 1 tablespoon of sugar at a time, beating well between each addition, and continue beating until you can no longer feel grains of sugar when you rub the mixture between your thumb and forefinger. Use a large metal spoon to transfer the mixture to the prepared baking sheet and smooth it out with a palette knife. You want a rectangle about 20 x 30 cm/8 x 12 inches and no thicker than 1 cm/½ inch.

Bake the meringue in the preheated oven for 20 minutes, until it is just set and the top turns a light caramel colour and is no longer sticky when lightly touched.

Take a second piece of baking parchment, slightly larger than the meringue, and sprinkle over 1 teaspoon caster/superfine sugar. Quickly flip the baking sheet upside-down so that the meringue is turned out onto the paper. Tap the bottom of the sheet so that the meringue comes away in one piece. Peel off the bottom piece of baking parchment. Firmly roll the meringue up into a log with the second sheet of paper and wrap in a clean tea/dish towel. Set aside to cool completely.

Put the cream and icing/confectioners' sugar in a bowl and whisk until firm peaks form. Unroll the meringue. Spoon the cream over the meringue, leaving a 2-cm/1-inch margin around the edge. Arrange the strawberries over the cream and roll up. Dust liberally with icing/confectioners' sugar and cut into thick slices to serve.

index

credits

recipes

Maxine Clark
apple & lemon sponge cake
apple, prune & armagnac crisp
apricot & almond slump
berry cobbler
blackberry cobbler
blueberry & lemon cobbler
buttered apricot betty
caramel apple crisp
chocolate, orange & date steamed pudding
bourbon pears with frangipane streusel
cherry clafoutis
blackberry & apple crumble
cranachan crumble
cranberry & apple cobbler
cranberry & orange streusel
drunken pear tart
free-form peach tart
gooseberry & ginger crumble
individual pear, maple & pecan cobblers
lemony apple crumble
little raspberry & rose cobblers
mango & coconut macaroon crisp
molasses banana cobbler
mulled mixed fruit crumble
nectarine & ginger crisp
peach & amaretti crisp
pear & chocolate crumble
pear, maple & pecan cobblers
pineapple rum betty with coconut
plum & hazelnut pandowdy
rhubarb & orange crumble
simple plum crumble
summer berry cobbler
toffee banana crumbles

Laura Washburn
apple & blackberry crumble
apple betty with dried cranberries
apple dappy
apple tart
baked plums in puff pastry
classic apple pie
Dutch apple pie
peach cobbler
pear & almond tart
pear & fig clafoutis
pear slump
praline apple strudel
spiced apple cake
tarte tatin

Ross Dobson
almond & orange syrup cake
apple & blueberry tarts
brioche pudding with blackberries
baked Granny Smith & blueberry pudding
blackberry crumble
cherry & almond clafoutis
cherry & ricotta strudel
dusky apple pie
fig & honey croissant pudding
fresh fig & walnut meringue
raspberry & almond tart
Moroccan apple pie
nectarine & pistachio summer crumble
peach & raspberry scone cake
pear & ginger crumble cake
pear, almond & mascarpone tart
strawberry buttermilk cake
strawberry meringue roulade
upside-down peach cake

Brian Glover
lemon & blackberry puddings
lemon, courgette & poppyseed cake

Caroline Marson
caramelized pear & cranberry tarts
upside-down apple cakes with ginger cream

Fiona Beckett
pear, Gorgonzola & pecan tartlets with maple drizzle

Tessa Bramley
raspberry & apple crispy cobbler

Tonia George
nutty plum crumble

photography

Key: bg = background

Martin Brigdale
Pages 20 inset, 119, 120, 142 inset

Peter Cassidy
Endpapers. pages 6 row 1: centre left & centre right, 6 row 2: left & centre left, 6 row 3: left, centre left, & right, 6 row 4: all, 7–11, 14, 15 inset, 16 inset, 17, 18, 19, 22, 23 inset, 24, 25, 29, 30, 31 inset, 32, 33, 34, 35 inset, 36–39, 40 inset, 41, 43 inset, 44, 46, 47 inset, 49, 50, 52 inset, 53–63, 64 inset, 65, 66, 67, 69, 70, 73, 74, 75 inset, 76 inset, 77, 79, 81 inset, 82, 83, 84, 86 bg, 87, 89, 96, 99, 100, 101, 102 inset, 106, 110, 114–117, 118 inset, 122 bg, 124–127, 129 inset, 131, 135, 144, 147, 149, 152, 153 inset, 157 bg, 158–160

Jean Cazals
Page 151

Lisa Cohen
Page 146 inset

Tara Fisher
Pages 86 inset, 133 inset

Christine Hanscomb
Page 45

Richard Jung
Pages 1, 2, 3 inset, 4, 5, 6 row 1: left, 6 row 2: centre right & right, 6 row 3: centre right, 12 inset, 13, 21, 68 bg, 71, 72 inset, 78, 80, 88, 90 inset, 91, 92, 94 inset, 95, 104, 112, 122 inset, 123, 128, 134, 136, 138 inset, 139, 140, 141, 143, 145, 148, 155, 156, 157 inset

William Lingwood
Pages 93 inset, 109 inset, 150 inset

David Munns
Pages 42, 132

© Steve Painter
Pages 98, 103

William Reavell
Pages 26, 27 inset, 68 inset, 113 inset, 137 inset

Claire Richardson
Page 154 inset

Kate Whitaker
Pages 3 bg, 12 bg, 15 bg, 16 bg, 20 bg, 23 bg, 27 bg, 28, 31 bg, 35 bg, 40 bg, 43 bg, 47 bg, 48, 51, 52 bg, 64 bg, 72 bg, 75 bg, 76 bg 81 bg, 85, 90 bg, 93 bg, 94 bg, 97, 102 bg, 105, 107, 108, 109 bg, 111, 113 bg, 118 bg, 121 bg, 129 bg, 130, 133 bg, 137 bg, 138 bg, 142 bg, 146 bg, 150 bg, 153 bg, 154 bg

Polly Wreford
Pages 6 row 1: right, 121 inset